SMOKE AND MIRRORS

Jaime Malamud-Goti

SMOKE AND MIRRORS

THE PARADOX OF THE DRUG WARS

Westview Press
BOULDER • SAN FRANCISCO • OXFORD

We acknowledge with gratitude Anna Crankshaw's contribution of illustrations for the text and cover.

All rights reserved. No part of this publication may be reproduced or transmitted in any form or by any means, electronic or mechanical, including photocopy, recording, or any information storage and retrieval system, without permission in writing from the publisher.

Copyright © 1992 by Westview Press, Inc., except illustrations, which are © by Anna Crankshaw

Published in 1992 in the United States of America by Westview Press, Inc., 5500 Central Avenue, Boulder, Colorado 80301-2847, and in the United Kingdom by Westview Press, 36 Lonsdale Road, Summertown, Oxford OX2 7EW

Library of Congress Cataloging-in-Publication Data
Malamud Goti, Jaime E.
  Smoke and mirrors : the paradox of the drug wars / by Jaime Malamud-Goti
    p. cm.
  Includes bibliographical references.
  ISBN 0-8133-1360-0
  1. Narcotics, Control of—Bolivia. 2. Narcotics, Control of—United States. 3. Coca industry—Bolivia—Chaparé. 4. Drug traffic—Bolivia. 5. United States. Drug Enforcement Administration.   I. Title.
HV5840.B6M35 1992
363.4'5'0984—dc20   91-17076
                                                                                     CIP

Printed and bound in the United States of America

∞ The paper used in this publication meets the requirements of the American National Standard for Permanence of Paper for Printed Library Materials Z39.48-1984.

10   9   8   7   6   5   4   3   2   1

To Libbet, Jaime, and Susana

Contents

Preface	ix
Acknowledgments	xix
List of Acronyms	xxi

    Introduction   1

    Notes, *6*

1 Coca Business in the Chapare   7

    1. Entering the Bolivian War on Drugs, *7*
    2. The Kollas, *9*
    3. The Cambas, *10*
    4. Changing Camba-Kolla Relations, *11*
    5. The Drug Business in the Chapare and Its Transformations, *12*
    6. The New Mode of Exchange, *15*
    7. The Effect of the Transformation on Kollas, *16*
    8. Conclusions, *19*
    Notes, *20*

2 Joint U.S.-Bolivian Enforcement and Eradication   27

    1. How to Protect Democracy: Recipes from the United States, *27*
    2. Operation Blast Furnace, *30*
    3. Drug Law Enforcers in 1990, *32*
    4. The Drug Enforcement Agency, *35*
    5. The Crop Eradication Effort, *37*
    6. Transformation Among Coca Producers, *38*

7. Shifts in U.S. Policy, *39*
8. Problems of Conflicting Interests: Santa Ana, *41*
9. Bombings in the Chapare, *43*
10. Summary, *44*
Notes, *45*

3 Huanchaca — 51

1. The Huanchaca Assassinations, *51*
2. The Investigation, *52*
3. More Scandalous Repercussions, *53*
4. In Conclusion, *58*
Notes, *59*

4 Bureaucracies at Their Worst — 63

1. The Appeal of Paradoxes, *63*
2. Who Is Cheating on Whom? *65*
3. If You Want to Succeed, Avoid Success, *67*
4. Who Wants to Bring the Good Old Army In? *70*
5. Some Conclusions, *81*
Notes, *83*

5 In the Realm of Paradoxes — 91

1. A Fresh Start, *91*
2. Bureaucracies at Work, *93*
3. The Singularity of Bolivia's "Corruption," *95*
4. Bolivia's Interagency Friction, *97*
5. "Clientelism," *97*
6. How U.S. and Bolivian Bureaucracies Interact, *98*
7. The Weight of Officials' Personal Interests, *99*
8. To Conclude, *101*
Notes, *101*

Postscript — 109

Notes, *111*

Selected Bibliography — 113
About the Book and Author — 117

Preface

Drugs seem to have a stronger impact on people than is often assumed. They seem to affect not only the psyche of the people who ingest them but also the minds of the professionals and officials who intend to control their production and use. My interest in drug policy in general, and in the Bolivian case in particular, stems from my experience as an official in the Alfonsin administration in Argentina who was affected by the drug war. As such, I was first introduced to the Bolivian cocaine war when I visited that country as an Argentinean envoy.

Argentina has not yet had to contend with opiates or any other kind of highly addictive substances, and so far, crack and meta-amphetamines are only legendary among the country's population. Except for some military sources that linked drug consumption to terrorist insurgency in the late 1970s and early 1980s, hardly any violent criminality has been attributed to drug use or traffic in that country. At the department for drug-related studies at the University of Buenos Aires,[1] which I once chaired, we hosted representatives of the main rehabilitation centers in Argentina, and it was clear that the number of drug addicts in Argentina was fairly small. Estimates revealed that there were no more than 30,000 compulsive consumers, most of whom alternated among a varied range of substances encompassing marijuana, cocaine, and chemicals such as barbiturates and codeine. Although there is a drug problem in Argentina, it is not crucial given the other social plights the country is facing: the growing infant mortality rate, childhood diseases, and a large variety of predicaments that are far more damaging than drug abuse. According to official estimates, for instance, the number of alcoholics soared in 1990 to over 1 million.

In spite of the relatively small amount of drug-related violence and consumption in Argentina, alarming news from Colombia, Peru, and the United States, and the influence of the U.S. Embassy, have brought the issue under the spotlight. In December 1990, there was hardly a page in the local newspapers that did not report on bombings in Medellín, shootouts in Miami, or the thousands of syringes picked up in the streets of Rome and Madrid. Newspapers invariably included several statements from top officials in President Carlos Saúl Menem's administration stating their view that drugs required more repression and warning of the threat that drugs posed to the Argentinean way of life. The official rhetoric had hardly any foundation—evidence indicated that the reality was less than apocalyptic—but there still was some reason for concern. In 1988, Juan Pirker, then chief of the Federal Police, had conveyed his fear that Colombian cartels could be attempting to make a breakthrough into Argentina, as a Colombian citizen allegedly involved in cocaine smuggling had been arrested in the outskirts of Buenos Aires. This case, however, in which Argentinean territory was used to try to transport cocaine to Europe, was not the prelude of an invasion of the Colombian cartels but seemingly an isolated episode. No serious violence was ever reported, and Luis Losada, the customs judge who investigated the case, told me that to his knowledge, it was the only case in which a Colombian organization had operated in Argentina.[2]

In 1990, the narcotics division of the Argentine Federal Police said it had discovered fewer cases of drug dealing and consumption than in the previous year, and although the National Gendarmerie, Argentina's border police, disagreed with this statement, its own appraisal did not reveal any substantial hike in drug-related activities. Nevertheless, the government stepped up a rhetoric that ceaselessly alluded to drugs as being a threat to "social survival" and "national security." Such a bleak, yet groundless, view was disputed by only a few scholars and even fewer judges. The administration's officials were trapped in a verbal crescendo that, by September 1990, would not stop short of calling drug dealers murderers, traitors, and other such epithets. Menem himself, who had declared that his humanitarian fiber was saddened by the idea that military officers convicted for human rights violations should remain in jail, believed that drug traffickers should be dealt with as traitors to Argentina and subjected to capital punishment.[3] In recent Argentinean history, the death penalty has only been invoked during military regimes and has not been applied by the judiciary since early in this century. It is also noteworthy that since 1984, the country has been bound by the San Jose de Costa Rica human rights accord, which bars new legislation that reinstates the death penalty.

The importance of fighting drugs was not Menem's invention. In a less vociferous, discreet manner, the issue was also promoted by President Raúl Alfonsin, inaugurated in December 1983 after a long period of authoritarian regimes. Pressed by U.S. diplomats who stressed that Argentina should cooperate more actively in the world's antidrug campaign, Alfonsin instructed me as his adviser to set up a commission to centralize government policies, and for over a year, I engaged in the frustrating task of elaborating policies that most officials thought were hardly important compared with the economic, health, institutional, and educational catastrophes the military had left behind. Looking back, they were right.

In July 1986, I was promoted to the rank of state secretary and moved back into my original advisory position, which largely consisted of human rights policies and legal issues that the president followed personally. Nonetheless, this redeployment did not remove me from dealing with drug policies, as one of my new responsibilities consisted of watching over the drug commission, which was now chaired by an under-secretary. I was still the highest-ranking executive officer in the field.

In late 1987, I was appointed solicitor to the Argentine Supreme Court, but my involvement in drug policies did not cease. By this time the president had upgraded the institutional standing of the drug issue by setting up a new commission, which he himself chaired. The minister of the interior and health and I were members of the commission. One of its priorities, set by Alfonsin, was to coordinate policies with neighboring countries. I thus talked to many of my Latin American colleagues, and from May through July 1988, we sought to achieve a series of bilateral agreements between neighboring countries. I met with the ministers of justice and the interior of Brazil and Uruguay, I organized meetings of our countries' top police officers, and in mid July, with the assistance of the Bolivian and Argentinean Foreign Affairs Ministries, I visited La Paz.

The timing of my visit could not have been more propitious, as momentous events were occurring in Bolivia. A harsh, doggedly disputed antidrug law (law 1008) had been enacted a few days before my arrival, and Roberto Suarez-Gomez, the famous Bolivian drug lord, fell into the hands of the special antidrug police.

To honor the new bonds between the two countries, and after I had spoken to the cabinet ministers with jurisdiction on the drug issue, the Argentinean ambassador held a luncheon at his residence, and among the guests were the ministers of foreign affairs, the interior, and agrarian and rural matters as well as the under-secretaries of social defense and alternative development. Just as I was receiving a copy of the new drug law from the interior minister, Juan Carlos Duran, Duran was called out of the room. When he returned, he proudly announced that Roberto Suarez-Gomez, famous for his offer to pay Bolivia's foreign debt (among other flamboyant gestures), had been arrested on his ranch in the northern territory of the Beni. After a brief silence, the luncheon regained its previous lively atmosphere; there were no visible signs of surprise or exhilaration. As I later learned, Suarez had already lost his leverage, and it was rumored that after being ostracized from the drug trade by his own comrades, he had arranged with the government to turn himself in.

The next day, I flew to Cochabamba, a valley town some 200 kilometers east of La Paz. The Bolivian government had sent Anibal Aguilar-Gomez, then under-secretary of alternative development, to escort me, and Juan Valle-Raleigh, an Argentinean diplomat serving in Bolivia, was the embassy's representative. Cochabamba is a small, picturesque colonial town. Blessed with dry, mild weather, its palm trees and flowery boulevards contrast with the grey overtones of the La Paz landscape. At the town's small airport, we were met by a considerable number of heavily armed security officers who would escort us in Jeeps on a tour of the Chapare tropics, the coca growing area that lies some 170 kilometers north of the city of Cochabamba. It was to be a one-day excursion consisting of a few hours' visit to the Chapare police outposts of Villa Tunari and Chimoré. From the latter, a DEA aircraft would transport Valle and me to the lowland city of Santa Cruz de la Sierra to finally travel back to La Paz that evening on a regular flight, as my wife and I were expected in the Argentinean province of Salta the next morning.

The ride to the Chapare jungle was indeed interesting. Leaving the city of Cochabamba, we drove up a high, dry mountain chain. At a spot high in the mountains, we stopped at a checkpoint where bus passengers congregated in a cold blizzard around policemen who thoroughly searched for any materials or utensils that could be used in cocaine paste manufacturing. Presumably to satisfy my curiosity, I was invited by Aguilar and a police officer into the shed where seized items were untidily stored, among them, toilet paper, kerosene lanterns, plastic sheets, car batteries, and tin drums. As Aguilar explained, these seemingly harmless articles are essential to the illicit drug industry. Car batteries contain badly needed sulfuric acid, the fuel inside the lanterns is a good solvent to precipitate the coca paste from the leaves, and toilet paper is used to dry the paste. I wondered what life would be like in the Chapare without toilet paper or kerosene, there being no electricity in that region.

As the road descended, the hills gradually turned green, and at the foot of the chain stretched the 2.5-million-hectare Chapare, the second largest coca generating region in the world (only the Huallaga Valley in Peru produces more). It must have been around noon when we arrived in Villa Tunari, the first police outpost in the Chapare. The view from there was extremely beautiful, as behind the high, green rain forest, the blackened peaks of the cordillera emerged between the clouds.

As we drove through the barbed wire that surrounds the barracks we were stunned to hear two loud bomb blasts. As we got out of the jeep, the commander of the outpost came to meet us with a solemn air. Wearing a combat uniform with two hand grenades hanging from his chest, he ushered us through the outpost to the edge of a river where men in speckled combat uniforms were preparing dynamite to blow up sulfuric acid. The rest of the encampment also seemed very active, with some men working out and others cleaning their weapons. Then a trooper came running toward us announcing that a coca paste carrier had been arrested a few yards away from the compound gates. Aguilar and the commander invited me to watch the proceedings, but as they walked toward the gate, I stayed behind. A man in plain clothes, who I learned was a local employee of the eradication office that was contiguous to the barracks, grinned at me, shaking his head: "It's the usual arrest show for visitors. The same man has been arrested at least ten times this year."

The visit to Chimoré, the main compound in the Chapare, also had its surprises. Leaving Villa Tunari, the main highway runs past Shinaota,[4] a shabby hamlet known to have been the center for major coca paste operations a few years back. The place still looked busy with ragged peasants walking on the side of the road, some carrying canisters and baskets. Standing in front of dark tin and wood hovels, barefoot children watched us ride by. Aguilar explained that minor drug transactions were still frequent in Shinaota despite its proximity to the police barracks and DEA agents in Chimoré.

Chimoré looked like an outpost in a war zone. The compound was surrounded by barbed wire, and a sentry emerged from behind a wall of sandbags to salute our convoy and lift the barrier to let us in. There were three helicopters sitting on landing platforms, and shots could be heard from a practice range farther away, behind an airstrip. U.S. personnel in combat apparel walked by in groups of two or three. These men were DEA agents, soldiers, and customs officials. The Bolivian commander of the unit took us for a walk around the site, and on this tour I was introduced to Dr. Enrique Valverde, the only visible civilian. In his mid-fifties, Valverde was the head of the State Department's Narcotics Assistance Unit (NAU) in the Cochabamba area. He was almost legendary in Cochabamba where his Quechua parents had brought him up. An incorruptible believer in the evil that cocaine means to Bolivia, Valverde had stood up against the military dictatorship of Luis Garcia-Meza and coordinated groups of civilian and military rebels. Valverde's staunchness on the drug issue (*pichicata*) had earned him enemies of all sorts and ranks. As I later grasped, he knew about my personal involvement in human rights in Argentina and was deeply interested in hearing about the trials of the generals in my country, which, to his mind, were among the greatest events of this century in South America.

Shortly after we were introduced, Valverde gently took me aside so that he would not be heard by the rest of the party. "Everything you see here is useless," he commented. "All the efforts to get this campaign going are hampered by corruption. You must get some of your police officers to come here and watch over what is going on. Perhaps our sense of shame will be helpful to us. There are no antidrug campaign casualties here; the few casualties reported as consequences of the war were the result of private fights over drug deals or jealous villagers in Shinaota avenging affairs with their wives." I promised Valverde to do my best to send policemen from Argentina, which I did once I got back to Buenos Aires with the enthusiastic backing of Chief Pirker. A few officers were sent, but after foreign service officials in Argentina expressed their fears about the international conflict such a step could bring about, the officers' mission was extremely constrained.

Around 4:30, we were on the road again. Anibal Aguilar had stayed behind in Chimoré, and the convoy escorted Valle-Raleigh and me to the airfield where the DEA aircraft was to pick us up to fly us to Santa Cruz. The airfield was literally surrounded by U.S. personnel with assault rifles, because, as someone explained, it was a "critical" area. The airplane had already landed three times but had had to take off each time after a three-minute wait—a security measure devised for critical areas. It was dusk, and the plane never came back, because Aguilar had not kept to the official schedule and it was too late to attempt another landing. We were taken back to Chimoré by our escort.

In Chimoré, U.S. officers tried in vain to make contact with the pilot, but he had gone back to Santa Cruz. With no better alternative, Aguilar decided to send us back to La Paz by Jeep. This time without extra protection, Valle-Raleigh and I were driven away in a Jeep by two police drivers. The policemen endured the bitter cold of the high mountains by chewing coca leaves. Wearing tropical clothes, we shivered ceaselessly from the lack of heating. We arrived in La Paz at 8 in the morning, one hour before my scheduled trip to Argentina.

The cold kept me from sleeping, but it gave me the opportunity to learn a few things from our police attendants, largely about the best way to chew coca in order to stay awake and to combat the freezing temperature. There was also gossip for entertainment. The commander of the first outpost we had visited, the drivers claimed, had made a fortune during his tenure in Villa Tunari. He had built a house in Cochabamba and had bought two brand-new cars. Nor was he an exception, and police posts in the Chapare were avidly disputed among officers—the outposts of Villa Tunari, Chimoré, and Ivirgarzama being among the best places to obtain wealth. The conversation went on, but as time elapsed, my attention began to dwindle as my fear of missing the flight grew stronger. We made it to the airport just on time after a few minutes' stop at the hotel where Libbet, my worried wife, had already packed. The policeman the minister of the interior had assigned to us was not there, despite my instructions, but Valle-Raleigh diligently took us to the airport.

There, the Argentinean ambassador, the under-secretary of social defense, and other officials waited to accompany my wife and me to the steps to the aircraft. Except for the Argentinean ambassador, with whom I had earlier established a very good relationship, the rest of the committee had solemn words to say about my visit. There ended my first and my only official trip to Bolivia.

At first sight, Bolivia's drug campaign was fraught with puzzles. Versions about the dangers of the Chapare were controversial: Although Valverde claimed that there had been no police casualties as a consequence of the cocaine war in the Chapare, Bolivian and U.S. authorities were acting as if the area were extremely dangerous. The hand grenades and the sandbags in Chimoré and Villa Tunari and the regulations that said the DEA airplane could remain on the ground for only three minutes seemed unnecessary. The situation was even more perplexing after the news that coca paste transactions still went on in villages only a few kilometers from the Bolivian police and the DEA outpost.

There were also different opinions about the arrest of Roberto Suarez-Gomez. Although high officials in La Paz declared his capture a victory over the Bolivian narcocracy, some police officers in the field perceived the arrest as part of a settlement between the administration and an aged, retired trafficker. Another account had it that Suarez was arrested mistakenly; the police were actually after another Suarez-Gomez—a much less renowned man but one with much more cocaine.

The point that caught my interest most, however, was not the distortions that wrapped up every story or the very often inexplicable behavior of the anticocaine personnel in the Chapare, but the seized utensils in the police shed. If mundane elements such as toilet paper, plastic sheets, and kerosene lanterns were an important part of the campaign, that campaign seemed to be doomed from its inception. Police efforts were centering on the most basic elements of ordinary communities in South America, and such an undertaking seemed directed against the communities themselves.

In September 1988, Libbet and I moved to the United States. Unfortunate immigration obstacles kept me from honoring a commitment to teach in Washington, D.C., so I then opted to apply for funds to go back to Bolivia and investigate the war on drugs in detail. The Harry-Frank

Guggenheim Foundation enabled me to conduct such research, which began in September 1989.

The investigation consisted of several trips to Bolivia. Each commenced in La Paz, where I spoke to Bolivian officials and politicians and U.S. diplomats and drug experts. In La Paz, the U.S. and Argentinean ambassadors to Bolivia were of incomparable help, and it would be unjust to allow my pessimism to blur their efforts in that country. I had heard President Alfonsin express high regard for U.S. Ambassador Robert Gelbard as being an extremely intelligent and staunchly democratic man with a strong interest in the welfare of Latin America, and my own opinion fully concurs with that assessment. The ambassador was friendly and generously shared with me his well-grounded knowledge of Latin America. Absorbed by the complicated role of representing his country's policies in the Southern Cone, he was far removed from the actual implementation of the antidrug campaign.

Argentinean Ambassador Eduardo Iglesias was also an extremely dedicated and able diplomat. Highly respected by the leaders of two consecutive administrations, he had many political and diplomatic friends in La Paz. Although critical of my contrived scholarly beliefs, his goodwill opened all possible doors for me.

On each trip I visited Cochabamba where I met with researchers, journalists, and police officers. From Cochabamba, I visited the Chapare, where access to sites that are often closed to other scholars was expedited by acquaintances from my July 1988 tour. Some of the officers were particularly helpful, and some of them took personal risks to widen my perception. Upon occasion, we visited outlying localities where we were met by distrustful, unfriendly faces. In other areas, we were welcomed amicably and invited to drink chicha (an Andean alcoholic beverage made from corn).

Some of the officers who accompanied me had long-lasting relationships with coca growers, stompers, and carriers. They were able to introduce me into what Dunkerley terms "the obscure, resistant-to-intrusion"[5] world in which cocaine is made. In this environment, friendship and enmity are divided by a very thin yet complicated line. There are cultural, family, and personal bonds that turn ought-to-be foes into allies; conversely, rivalries often stem from regional and family feuds. Among kin or peasants of the same culture, conflict often derives from different adaptive strategies to the new environment of the coca/cocaine industry.

Culture plays an essential role that often overrides duties that stem from holding public office. In January 1990, I met in La Paz an Aymara Indian and former high official who related to me a hair-raising story of split loyalties. Considering him one of their own, Aymara coca growers from a region called Yungas de La Paz confided in this man their plan to assassinate a group of police officers whose abuses and pillage had made their lives unbearable. Fearing that retaliation on the growers would result if he revealed his secret, the then member of the Bolivian administration chose not to report the conspiracy. As a consequence, several police officers were ambushed and killed a few weeks later.[6] Although it was the first time I had talked with this man, there were no signs of repentance or shame. His deepest conviction must have been that that was how it had to be.

Jaime Malamud-Goti

NOTES

1. Postgraduate Institute on Drug Abuse, University of Buenos Aires. I chaired the institute from its creation in 1986 to 1990.

2. Meeting with Losada in Buenos Aires on September 1, 1989.

3. See *Buenos Aires Herald*, August 3, 1989.

4. Like most villages in the Chapare, Shinaota has different names. Some call the hamlet Chinaota, Cinaota, or Chinahuata.

5. James Dunkerley, *Rebellion in the Veins: Political Struggle in Bolivia, 1952–1982* (London: Verso, 1984).

6. I met with him in a La Paz bar on January 8, 1990. He had been a member of Victor Paz-Estenssoro's administration (1985–1989).

Acknowledgments

This book was made possible by the Harry-Frank Guggenheim Foundation, an institution that made everything relaxed and agreeable. I am particularly indebted to Karen Colvard, the Guggenheim's Program Officer, who took an interest in my work however confusing it may have been in the early stages. I owe her my deepest gratitude.

In Bolivia, I obtained incomparable help from U.S. Ambassador Robert Gelbard and Argentinean Ambassador Eduardo Iglesias. Both offered me generous and friendly help and opened doors that were essential to the outcome of my work (with which they are likely to thoroughly disagree). I also got very useful ideas and suggestions from Dr. Roger Cortez, a former Bolivian congressman and a brilliant journalist who spent endless hours supplying me with materials and ideas. I am deeply thankful to Dr. Enrique Valverde with whom I spent endless hours in the bush gazing at the cordillera, traveling to exotic places, and talking to the most interesting characters in the Chapare.

In the Argentine Foreign Ministry, Roberto Pallarino and Juan Valle-Raleigh exhibited selfless interest in the subject by furnishing me with invaluable data. Valle also endured courageously the hardships of a nighttime crossing of the high mountains on my first visit to the Chapare.

Among U.S. friends and colleagues, I was helped by field visits and discussions with Bruce Perlman, Peter Lupsha, and Peter De Vasto. Invaluable suggestions were made to me about early drafts of the manuscript by Robert Murphy and Barbara Price of Columbia University's Anthropology Department. Roberto De Michele and Patricia Azzi also donated invaluable time. Monica Von Thun Calderon discussed with me many of my ideas and provided a strong source of stimulation. So has Larry Liftschultz, who patiently read the earliest drafts and made key suggestions.

My wife, Libbet Crandon-Malamud, advised me on an infinity of topics and ideas. Libbet also gave up much of her own time to guide me in the world of field research, and she later improved the strange, captivating, and curious language this book is written in. Megan Schoeck, my Westview Press copy editor, made further suggestions that I gratefully accepted.

There are many other people and groups to thank, including the U.S. Immigration and Naturalization Service. Had it not been for its bureaucratic, dogged attachment to forms that barred me from employment in the United States, I would have honored an agreement to teach at American University and thereby missed an excellent opportunity to write this book.

J. M-G.

Acronyms

ADN	Acción Democrática Nacionalista (a right-wing party)
COB	Corporacion Obrera Boliviana (Bolivian Workers' Corporation; the top trade unions organization)
CONALID	Consejo Nacional del Trafico Ilicito y Uso Indebido de Drogas (National Council for Illicit Traffic and Undue Consumption of Drugs)
DEA	Drug Enforcement Administration, U.S. Justice Department
DIRECO	Dirección de Reconversión de la Coca
DOD	U.S. Department of Defense
INM	International Narcotic Matters
Leopardos	*See* UMOPAR
MIR	Movimiento de Izquierda Revolucionaria (the Left Revolutionary Movement)
MNR	Movimiento Nacionalista Revolucionario
NAU	Narcotics Assistance Unit (a U.S. agency financing enforcement operations and in charge of crop eradication in Bolivia)
PIDYS	Proyecto Integral de Desarrollo y Substitución (Integral Project of Development and Substitution)
UMOPAR	Unidad Mobil de Patrullaje Rural (Mobile Unit of Rural Patrol; Bolivian police division specializing in drug enforcement in rural areas; members are also called Leopardos)
USAID	U.S. Agency for International Development

Introduction

Bolivia is a landlocked country of roughly 1 million square kilometers (424,000 square miles). It borders Argentina and Paraguay on the south, Brazil on the east and north, and Chile and Peru on the west. About two-thirds of the country's population inhabits the western third of the country: the altiplano, mountains, and high valleys. Almost in the center of the country sits the city of Santa Cruz de la Sierra. The Departamento de Santa Cruz is mostly flatland that stretches to the Departamentos del Beni and Cochabamba to the west. East of La Paz is the Departamento of Cochabamba, which stretches from its southern valleys through a sector of the cordillera and into the low rain forest. The rain forest of the Departamento of Cochabamba is the largest coca growing area in the country and is commonly known as the Chapare. The Chapare area includes the three provinces of the Chapare, Carrasco, and Tiraque. North of these provinces lies the Parque Nacional Isiboro Secure, a political invention of a military ruler in the 1960s, General René Barrientos, who decided to have this territory administered by La Paz as an effective way to terminate territorial conflicts between the Departamentos of Santa Cruz and Cochabamba. The idea did not prove entirely successful, however, because today a conflict of boundaries persists among Isiboro, Cochabamba, and Santa Cruz. In the late 1980s, around 10,000 hectares of coca were grown in Isiboro Secure.

In the north of Bolivia lie the Departamentos de Pando and the Beni, which borders Santa Cruz to the east. Pando is mostly impenetrable jungle, and it is said that Peruvian Shining Path guerrillas have established cantonments there. Although partly covered by high rain forest, the Beni's warm savannahs are natural cattle land. Except for some isolated Amazon tribes, the Beni is inhabited by recent migrants from Santa

Cruz de la Sierra, and family links between Benianos and Cruceños are very common. In fact, most cocaine traffickers own property in both departments.

Since the 1980s, the process of cocaine manufacturing in Bolivia has been carried out mostly by the 250,000–300,000 peasants in the Chapare and Isiboro areas. Most coca growers, between 80 percent and 90 percent according to the experts, also make coca paste, the first stage of the cocaine processing procedure. As Edmundo Morales explains, the transformation of the leaf into a mushy substance (coca paste) is accomplished in three stages using sulfuric acid, kerosene, and sodium carbonate or their substitutes.[1] Pit laborers stomp the leaves as they float on water, and sulfuric acid is then poured into holes in the ground. The bottoms of these pits are rendered watertight with plastic sheets, and plastic sheets are also utilized as shades at the sides of the pits to protect the contents from the dirt that drifts with the breeze. The resulting "broth" (*caldo*)[2] is treated with an alkaloid, normally sodium carbonate. After mixing the broth and the alkaloid, the base is stirred into a "soup," which is later mixed with a solvent, normally kerosene. The result of this treatment is the precipitation of a mushy substance that is then dried in the sun. This operation is usually sped up with paper, usually toilet paper.

The transformation of coca paste into cocaine hydrochloride is not done by the peasants, because this final process of refining cocaine is relatively complicated. It requires electricity, special presses, ether acetone, and more sophisticated anticorrosive containers such as porcelain vases; thus, it also requires capital. Cocaine hydrochloride is known to be produced on a large scale in hidden spots in the Beni and Santa Cruz. From those localities, cocaine has traditionally been transported to Colombia, but recent reports claim that the Colombians have been partly displaced by Brazilian drug rings and also that some Bolivian organizations have dared to sidestep both to smuggle the drug into Europe, mostly through Spain. There are exceptions to this large-scale production, however. It is said that some families manufacture cocaine hydrochloride in their homes in the towns of Santa Cruz and Cochabamba, and in the 1960s, a man called "the Nobel Laureate" because of his ingenuity and chemical abilities managed to refine cocaine for a group of friends behind the altar of Cochabamba's prison chapel.[3]

Bolivia is second only to Peru in coca production and supplies around 40 percent of the world's supply. Estimates about the size of the country's coca and cocaine production vary dramatically; even official Bolivian and foreign agencies have different figures. Henry Oporto-Castro claims that 70,000 hectares are used to grow coca in Bolivia and that the yield amounts to 132,400 tons of leaf.[4] It takes 100 kilos of leaf to get 4–4.5

kilos of coca paste, and 50 percent of the volume of the coca paste is lost when it is refined into cocaine hydrochloride.

The large profits obtained from the hydrochloride business benefit only a few. Around 200 families collected between 80 percent and 90 percent of the $2 billion Bolivia's cocaine yielded in 1985, and less than 15 percent of that amount remained in the country.[5] Knowledgeable sources claim that Bolivia's cocaine production increased almost 100 percent between 1985 and 1990, and Humberto Campodónico asserts that although Bolivia produces 40–45 percent of the cocaine in the world and Peru 50 percent, only 5–10 percent of the cocaine in the United States originates in Peru and 15 percent in Bolivia.[6]

It is calculated that 6–8 percent of Bolivia's 6 million inhabitants is directly connected with the coca/cocaine industry, and a much larger sector, of course, has a vested interest in the drug economy. The data available on coca and cocaine are controversial and vary with the sharp oscillations of the market price. At the beginning of February 1990, the word that circulated in La Paz was that growers were leaving the Chapare because the price of coca was so low that not even paste was profitable enough to make a living. A few days later, I found out in the Chapare that the value of coca had increased over a hundredfold. This intriguing economy does not allow accurate assessments of any sort, but many of its ups and downs may be inferred from the stories and explanations provided in this book. Other aspects remain a mystery to me, and I presume that there are riddles the governments of Bolivia and the United States, and even the cocaine dealers themselves, do not understand.

Opinions in the United States about the "war on drugs" are split. Although most of the scholars who study the subject demonstrate the war's deficiencies from the point of view of economics, civil liberties, international relations, and so on, official rhetoric has chosen a different tack. In the United States, politicians generally seem to have chosen to overlook the host of reasons why the current approach is not working and to advocate for more of the same, meaning investment in more resources, better training of enforcers, an increased presence of local and U.S. armed forces, and tougher controls against corruption.

The Bolivian case exposes the multiple inadequacies of the war on drugs, but does not suggest that the war is unsuccessful because the allotted resources are insufficient. Rather, it indicates that the eradication and enforcement programs are wrongly conceived. A brief account of the incidents that the drug repression in Bolivia has brought about raises questions about the nature of the approach adopted, and I will show that calling the effort a war entails distorting the image of the protagonists involved and the interests those agents embody. War implies a win/lose proposition that precludes an understanding of the large diversity of groups and the multiplication of interests that bear directly on the cocaine issue. Moreover, "war" means that the people involved are struggling in the interest of the party they represent—the United States or Bolivia in this particular case.

In dealing with the drug trade in Bolivia, U.S. politicians and policymakers have misleadingly identified three broad sectors as being involved in the conflict: (1) the government, its police force, and the military who seek to eradicate coca and control cocaine traffic, granting that a number of the officials play a part or have a vested interest in the drug traffic; (2) cocaine traffickers and a host of confederates such as financiers, suppliers of materials, and couriers, who are considered as the cocaine enemy; and (3) the campesino coca growers, a poor sector of nearly 400,000 inhabitants in need of protection in the struggle to survive. No distinctions are made concerning the U.S. participants, and it is assumed that diplomats, DEA and border patrol agents, soldiers, and civil servants in Bolivia devote all their efforts to serving the country's general interest, whatever that might mean. The brief story of drug enforcement in postdictatorial Bolivia that I present in this book will show the complexity of the players and how enforcement has had the paradoxical effect of enhancing the cocaine trade in that country. It will also show how sectorial bureaucratic interests and personal goals countervail all efforts to curb the drug traffic reduce coca growing, and, consequently, change the Bolivian economy.

To date, pressure from First World countries has not effected a decrease in the consumption of cocaine made from Bolivia's coca crop. Campaigns urged and aided by the First World to eradicate or substitute other crops for coca and to enforce laws against cocaine manufacturing, the U.S. war on drugs in particular, have proved fruitless.[7] In fact, Bolivian officials estimate that the amount of land dedicated to coca growing in the Chapare region alone has increased by 30 percent from 1987 to 1990.

Bolivia's domestic policies concerning coca and cocaine during the contemporary democratic period have varied from a laissez-faire stance to mounting major enforcement campaigns involving army units[8] to fight the cocaine traffic and calling in foreign troops to destroy laboratories and clandestine airfields.[9] Drastic measures that have earned approval from abroad have met with an equivalent amount of domestic rejection from peasants, political parties, and trade unions.[10]

The country's failure to come to grips with a predominant activity that undermines Bolivia's economy and institutions is owing not only to economic factors but to political and ideological ones as well. The lack of coercive power of the Bolivian state[11] and the multiplicity of interests that revolve around the drug trade make the present approach to the problem implausible at best. The very conception of the present war on drugs does not take into account the number of conflicting interests in Bolivia that originate in a multiplicity of sources, ranging from diverse cultures that maintain relationships of mutual antagonism, to the conflicting ambitions of over fifty political parties, to the vulnerability of the centralized state to partisan policy and privilege. The diversity of goals pursued by the U.S. policymakers, the different bureaucratic interests, and individual pursuits are not only neglected by the war approach, to a large extent they are a product of this conception. The proposition that an effective drug policy can be developed only after the array of Bolivian interests has been consulted is supported by the failure of the present policy and the strength of the government opposition groups that define Bolivian politics. At present, the diversity of these interests is not a part of the picture that is conveyed by Bolivian, U.S., and European politicians and policymakers.

In light of this hypothesis the war approach is not only inappropriate but inevitably doomed to fail. There are at least four reasons deriving from the complexity of the interests at stake that make the war on drugs in Bolivia implausible. First, the plethora of actively rivaling political parties and interest groups means that a "war" at less than an unbearable cost is impossible and that even consensus is infeasible without some compromise. Second, there is a lack of sufficiently coercive state institutions, both national and foreign, and any attempt to make the policing agencies more effective by increasing the number of national and foreign agents is self-defeating. In Bolivia, the state is too weak to keep a grip on its police, as the antidrug police force demonstrated when it abducted its founder, President Hernan Siles-Suazo on June 30, 1984. As foreign bureaucracies operating in Bolivia grow larger, so does the weight of their own bureaucratic interests in policy implementation. Third, the "illegal" sector is too large to be excluded from joint, concerted policies. Given that to varying degrees the country's economic and political life revolves around the cocaine trade, only by achieving a high degree of consensus will it be possible to produce an economic and institutional shift. Fourth, the lack of accepted parameters, and thus of a unified account of the country's situation—that is, the absence of any mechanism to achieve consensus—means that a high degree of compromise is necessary if an effective policy is to be developed.

This book will show how and why the current approach causes paradoxical behavior among U.S. officials and agents. Although normal in any national administration, the bureaucratic pursuances and inadequacies, and the furtherance of personal interests, are significantly enhanced by the current situation. I will attempt to demonstrate the flaws and dilemmas that the war on drugs policy has generated and to show that structural mutations are required to tackle the coca/cocaine issue if any improvement in drug consumption in the First World can be expected.

NOTES

1. Edmundo Morales, *Cocaine* (Tucson: University of Arizona Press, 1989), p. 71.

2. Ibid., p. 76.

3. This story was told to me by Enrique Valverde, whom I interviewed on May 30, 1990. Valverde was the head of the U.S. State Department's NAU in Cochabamba until 1990. The "Laureate" had joined a small club of cocaine manufacturers and consumers in Cochabamba in the mid-1960s. There were only fifteen or twenty members, and there was no attempt to expand the circle. The first time the police found cocaine, they did not know what to do about it as there were no criminal provisions regarding it.

4. Henry Oporto-Castro, "Bolivia: El complejo coca-cocaina," in *Coca, cocaina, y narcotráfico: Laberinto en los Andes*, ed. Diego García-Sayán (Lima: Comisión Andina de Juristas, 1989), p. 171. Humberto Campodónico agrees with Oporto as to the extent of cultivation, estimating that the size of the coca leaf yield is between 100,000 tons and 150,000 tons (Humberto Campodónico, "La política del aveztruz," in ibid., p. 223).

5. Samuel Doria-Medina, *La economia informal en Bolivia* (La Paz: Editorial Offset Boliviana Limitada, 1986), p. 70.

6. Campodónico, "La política del aveztruz," p. 223.

7. It is calculated that approximately 45 percent of the INM (International Narcotics Matters) money in producing countries is allotted to crop eradication, 35 percent is for interdiction, and less than 4 percent is for crop substitution and development (see Peter Andreas and Coletta Youngers, "U.S. Drug Policy and the Andean Cocaine Industry," *World Policy Journal* [1989], pp. 529–562).

8. For example, see *Latinamerica Press*, December 20, 1984.

9. "Operation Blast Furnace," Gendarmeria Nacional Argentina, internal report of Commanders Jorge Vazquez and Ricardo Lopez (note 7, supra).

10. The Villa Tunari incident (June 1988), in which about twenty campesinos died, was kindled largely because of the presence of foreign forces in the Chapare (interviews with Roger Cortez, journalist Elva Morales, Cochabamba, January 15, 1990; and Enrique Valverde, Cochabamba, January 14, 1990).

11. See James M. Malloy, "Authoritarianism and Corporatism: The Case of Bolivia," in *Authoritarianism and Corporatism in Latin America*, ed. James M. Malloy (Pittsburgh: University of Pittsburgh Press, 1979), p. 459.

1

Coca Business in the Chapare

Why did the Virgin Mary chew coca?

Because she was grieving for her son Jesus. She had lost him, her Jesus of Nazareth, born in the town of Jerusalem. There, when her son grew up and she began to lose him, she would cry for him and, in her infinite sorrow, she would chew some leaves of this bush. That is why it has become a consolation for all, why we chew it when we are sad.

—Extract from a taped conversation with
an eighty-six-year-old peasant from
a small village near Cuzco in the Peruvian Andes,
Latinamerica Press, December 1, 1983

1. ENTERING THE BOLIVIAN WAR ON DRUGS

After a forty-minute ride out of the temperate-weather town of Cochabamba, the road to the Chapare rain forest leads up to a cold plateau over 4,000 meters high. The UMOPAR police driver points his finger at the army barracks standing on the left-hand side and asks if you find something bizarre about the military constructions surrounded by a high wire fence. You notice that the buildings' walls are camouflaged with green and brown spots, but there does not seem to be anything exceptional about the compound. The driver exposes your lack of perception by pointing out that the camouflage paint does not cover the roofs of the buildings. You don't have to be a strategist to start wondering why anybody would want to camouflage the walls and not the tops of barracks in the middle of the Andes.

Two hours later, you gradually descend into the jungle. It is the hot, damp morning of January 16, 1990, and accompanied by a Bolivian NAU official, you are being driven by a Leopardo (UMOPAR police officer) into the UMOPAR/DEA compound of Chimoré in the Chapare rain forest. As the vehicle approaches the barbed wire that surrounds the encampment, two men in fatigues solemnly salute you while a third trooper, with a rifle hanging on his back, lifts the gate to let you into the outpost. You ride past what seem to be troopers' dormitories on both sides of the road, some of which are almost covered by sandbags. Half a mile inside the outpost you discover three Huey helicopters standing on cement platforms, and about a quarter of a kilometer to your right there is a group of thirty or forty men working on a runway. The driver takes you near, and you realize that two of the men are handcuffed. The rest are busily carrying lumber and heaps of mud in rusty wheelbarrows.

With uncontrollable curiosity you ask about these men, and your companion explains that they are inmates from a prison run by "Idi Amin," a heavy black man whose real name is Martin Gira. Gira runs the so-called rehabilitation camp with unusual brutality. The NAU official gets off the lorry and engages in a conversation with Idi Amin, who has briskly approached him to shake hands. Both men start talking, gesticulating exuberantly, turning ceaselessly, waving their arms, and pointing in all directions. The driver then turns around to you and explains that the next day very high officials from the United States, perhaps even senators, will visit the barracks. The commander of the Leopardos, the antidrug police, is planning to honor his guests with one of his favorite demonstrations, burning coca paste. With an air of confidentiality, the driver goes on to explain that several times a year, Idi Amin brings in his men to build a pile of mud with firewood underneath it. An hour later, when the prisoners have left, two Leopardos will cover the mud with a thin layer of grey mush, coca paste. Although this undertaking goes far beyond Amin's duties, he is delighted to contribute to the image of his son's father-in-law, a Bolivian drug enforcement official serving in the region.

The three helicopters take off and fly above your head in circles before finally heading north. "They are off to bring the 'senators,'" the UMOPAR driver explains. Two days later you read in a Cochabamba newspaper that U.S. officials burned a large amount of cocaine after eating lunch at the UMOPAR headquarters in Chimoré. There is a photograph in the La Paz newspaper *Ultima Hora*[1] showing Congressmen Bob Wise and Al McCandless setting fire to "1,633 kilos of cocaine sulphate."[2] You know it was mostly mud, but for unskilled witnesses, the smell of the burning mud seems like coca because it has been "seasoned" for special guests. You have been introduced to the world of the war on drugs in Bolivia.

That war is taking place in a complex social setting, and an oversimplified warlike approach to solving conflicts often conceals that complexity. Policymakers and witnesses of the Andean cocaine situation often insist on isolating drug traffickers from the social environment in which they operate. To make the strategy fit the environment, antidrug violence is portrayed as the (justified) means that decent citizens of the United States and Bolivia resort to to defend themselves against a well-defined group of criminals. James E. Inciardi, an exponent of this view, describes Bolivia's capital, La Paz, as a city with "a small population of financial elites— merchants, professionals, and politicians who see to the needs of the city and the country; executives and landowners made affluent by Bolivia's rich mineral resources; and 'narcotraficantes,' whose extravagant wealth has come from the cultivation of the drug leaf and its processing into cocaine."[3] Inciardi seems to overlook the fact that the time of the tin magnates is long gone. Since their mines were taken over by the state in 1952, tin has never been profitable and making fortunes out of this mineral is far from simple. But what is really misleading is the way the author classifies Bolivians. Nobody with any curiosity who has visited Bolivia would venture to separate landowners from politicians, or politicians from merchants. Above all, no one would isolate any of these sectors from cocaine traffickers. The only clear distinction in the Bolivian social environment is one that Inciardi overlooks: Only the Aymara and the Quechua Indians from the Andes engage in coca growing; traffickers never do.[4]

In this first chapter, I provide a sketch of the social actors in the coca/cocaine business in the Chapare and the dynamics of their connections. As the sector of Bolivia where most of the coca that pours into the cocaine market is grown and partly processed, the Chapare provides a suitable place for a look at the variety of actors involved in the coca/cocaine economy.

2. THE KOLLAS

Until the beginning of the cocaine boom in the late 1970s, the Chapare region of Bolivia was a sparsely populated area that supported bands of hunters and gatherers and a few peasant migrants from the highlands. By the 1980s, the population had swollen to more than 300,000—a sizable figure for a country with barely 6 million people and an increase of over 240,000 in less than ten years. This sudden surge in population has led to unprecedented economic and social exploitation, environmental degradation, and violence. One writer argues that it has resulted in the greatest devastation in Bolivian history,[5] yet there are decisive economic incentives in the Chapare. For many Bolivian highlanders, it is the spot to seek cash;

for some lowlanders, the Chapare is the first link of a business chain leading to enormous profits.

The fall of the international market prices of tin and gas in the 1970s and 1980s led to the demise of the highland economy and staggering unemployment among the Kollas, the people of the highlands,[6] and stimulated migration to the Chapare. There were other reasons for this migration, as well, including cultural ones. A number of Aymara and Quechua Indians who had given up their traditional family life in the highlands, for one reason or another found that returning to their native communities and reestablishing functional traditional family ties was extremely difficult. Carlos Dipp, Bolivian President Jaime Paz-Zamora's under-secretary for treatment of drug abuse, believes that military service has played a prime role in this regard. Army ex-conscripts, 90 percent of whom are peasants or mestizos, are flatly rejected by their original communities, because the traits they acquired in the service alienate them from their original social environment, yet there are few choices available to these individuals outside the Ayllu or kin-based system of production in the highlands.[7] In addition, as one of the poorest countries in the hemisphere, Bolivia's formal economy has very little to offer, and the informal economy is flooded. Thus, the Chapare also became a compelling alternative for laid-off miners from Potosí and Oruro and drought-stricken peasants of the Cochabamba Valley.

3. THE CAMBAS

The collapse of the cotton market in 1975 and 1976 was a decisive event for the Cambas, the settlers in the Bolivian lowlands who are allegedly of Spanish descent. Inexperienced cotton growers who had obtained easy loans were forced to export their cotton at a time when the international prices were depressed, and large parts of the cotton production wound up unsold in an attempt to avoid untimely sales.[8] Coupled with business mismanagement, the subsequent loss of international markets drove the industry into bankruptcy, which pushed the wealthy Santa Cruz cotton producers into looking for a more lucrative enterprise.[9] The enterprise of choice was cocaine hydrochloride, which required the immediate development and organization of coca cultivation in the Chapare.

The Cambas offered immediate cash for such work, which was an attractive alternative to unemployment or overwhelming crop failure. Between 1975 and 1982, most of the first stage of cocaine manufacturing, stomping coca paste, was carried out by Kolla labor in Montero, north of the city of Santa Cruz,[10] and then this activity was increasingly moved into the growing area, the Chapare. Thus, the cocaine boom was spawned through the use of primarily Kolla labor in coca production.

4. CHANGING CAMBA-KOLLA RELATIONS

Until the 1980s, only a few families in the Chapare region were involved in the production of coca paste, the first step in the manufacturing of cocaine hydrochloride, as the industry was then primarily a venture for underground networks that operated largely in the departments of Santa Cruz and the Beni. Kollas would sell their coca leaf to *zepes* ("ants," or Kolla carriers) in the eastern lowlands, and the *zepes* carried the leaf from the Chapare to the Santa Cruz region where it was stomped under Camba supervision by Kolla migrants to that area. The money gained by the stompers and paste dealers at that time was spent principally in Santa Cruz.

The pattern changed when, in 1982, peasant "cooperatives" in the Chapare villages of Sinahota and Ivirgarzama undertook to process the paste themselves and sell it to the traffickers' organizations to be refined into cocaine hydrochloride for export.[11] At first, the cooperatives consisted of a few peasants, but the 1983 drought, mine closures, and spiraling unemployment in the highlands and valleys pushed thousands of peasants in the Chapare and into coca paste production,[12] so that by 1986, numerous Kolla families were producing the paste as a cottage industry. Today, most land-based peasants in the Chapare smuggle or purchase smuggled kerosene and sulfuric acid to produce cocaine sulphate. Thus, the Chapare has become the spot where coca paste is produced by Kolla labor to be sold to Camba traffickers, with the exception of a small portion that is turned into *pitucos* (cocaine-paste cigarettes) for consumers in the region.[13]

The increase of paste manufacturing in the Chapare since the early 1980s has led some experts on Bolivia to claim that this enterprise by growers constitutes a victory for the peasant settlers in the region, as the coca growers have been able to obtain a more important role in the Camba coca/cocaine business.[14] Although there are some more innovative settlers in areas like Chimoré who are willing to associate with the Camba cocaine traffickers,[15] there are clear signs that no actual "democratization" of the trade has occurred. The poverty of the region's inhabitants and the lack of sophistication of paste production are clear indications that this new involvement of Kolla peasant growers in the illicit cocaine business has not led to any upward mobility of the campesinos. On the contrary, it represents a transformation from a viable peasant economy based on reciprocity and barter to one of dependency on the cash market. The Camba traffickers' economy actually perpetuates poverty in the Chapare because the Camba organizations in Santa Cruz and the Beni have enough economic clout to define the conditions under which purchases from the Kolla growers will be carried out. Furthermore, since enforcement is largely being concentrated on the small coca paste producer, the Cambas have shifted the weight of repression onto the Kollas by forcing them to produce the coca paste and transport it to pickup centers.[16]

5. THE DRUG BUSINESS IN THE CHAPARE AND ITS TRANSFORMATIONS

Coca paste manufacturing in the Chapare today is extremely unsophisticated. The variety of items used in the process and seized to avert it are essential to everyday life in any vast, poor section of Latin America: fuel tanks, metal drums, plastic sheets, car batteries, kerosene lanterns, and toilet paper.[17] A few growers have their own cement *secaderos* (drying platforms); the rest dry their leaf wherever they can (consequently, some back roads are covered with drying coca leaf).

The extent to which coca growing and processing expanded in the mid-1980s in the Chapare is illustrated by the San Miguel episode in 1984. The executive director of the secretariate for tropical development, Carlos Montaño, toured the Chapare with USAID personnel to encourage local residents to build schools and sanitation facilities. Checks had been issued through the village peasant unions[18] to build such utilities on the condition that they be ready by a certain date. Most of the pledges were not met, but in the hamlet of San Miguel a small building to serve as a school was surprisingly ready when Montaño and his USAID party arrived to examine the villagers' accomplishments. Speeches were given to celebrate its inauguration, but when the doors of the school were opened to display the interior, there were no desks or blackboards inside the school, and the floor was covered with drying coca.[19] The episode must have warned Montaño of the use *cocaleros* (coca growers) would make of new facilities and made him realize that any improvement in the area's living conditions was likely to serve the coca growing economy.[20] Thus, Montaño came to firmly believe that investments should be made outside of the Chapare and that any attempt to dissuade further coca/cocaine activities would have to involve attracting peasants away from the Chapare region.[21]

There are two closely interrelated reasons for the current state of drug production in the Chapare. The first is the prevalence and nature of the market economy of the eastern lowland Cambas; the second lies in the nature of the coca/cocaine repression in Bolivia. Kollas in the Chapare engage in paste manufacturing because both the official enforcement policy and the prevailing Camba economic strategy compel them to. The approach jointly adopted by the U.S. and Bolivian administrations to discourage the cultivation of coca periodically depresses the market price of the leaf—which is also legally consumed—to below production costs.[22] Coca prices have frequently dropped to such an extent that they cannot sustain the producer, which forces peasant coca agriculturalists into the cottage paste industry in order to make a living.[23]

Until the early 1980s, witnesses assert,[24] the heads of the traffickers' organizations themselves spent time in the Chapare. In the mid-1970s, at the beginning of the cocaine boom, they organized encampments where coca leaf was gathered to be later ferried to the regions of the Beni and Santa Cruz. The leaf was transported on airplanes, trucks, and boats. The heads of traffickers' organizations from Santa Cruz, Jorge Roca, known as Techo de Paja (straw roof—referring to his blond hair), and Roberto Suarez-Gomez, from the Beni, often visited the Chapare localities of Villa Tunari, Eterazama, and Ivirgarzama. The then director of the Dirección de Reconversión de la Coca, Carlos Arauz, and the NAU[25] agent in Cochabamba, Enrique Valverde, recall their dread when they stumbled across one of them. On a visit to the Ivirgarzama police compound, Arauz and Valverde encountered Techo de Paja and his army of bodyguards as they were leaving the site after a business visit to the commandant. Arauz and Valverde took to their heels and so did Techo de Paja and his crew, each of them thinking that they were being chased by the other.[26]

In those early days of the cocaine business, the famous Roberto Suarez-Gomez was also a frequent visitor to the Chapare—famous because he had made the world's front pages when he offered to pay Bolivia's foreign debt in cash in exchange for immunity to run his cocaine business. Suarez leased a hotel, La Pozas, near Villa Tunari so he could mix business and pleasure with his closest collaborators during the carnival of 1980, and although he did not have a reputation for being cruel, this sojourn in the Chapare had a deplorable finale, the assassination of Benjamin Cortez, the owner of the hotel. Cortez had threatened to report his guests to the police when they refused to pay their hotel bill,[27] and he was found shot the next day at his ranch just up the road from the hotel.[28]

When Cambas began to teach Chapareños how to make coca paste in the early 1980s and coca stomping began to spread in the Chapare, the heads of the Camba traffickers' organizations gradually disappeared from the area. Only lieutenants visited the Chapare to supervise the new organizational style that the business had acquired, and the Camba networks were concerned with making the arrangements for the smuggling of needed materials into the Chapare and setting up a brokerage system to make pickups of the paste more concentrated. These moves saved costs and reduced risk in an increasingly dangerous area. In 1983, the new special antidrug police corps, the UMOPAR,[29] was created,[30] and in 1984, the military took over the Chapare on orders from President Siles-Suazo. Although the enforcers were inefficient and largely corruptible, it was still safer for the Cambas to delegate the first stages of the drug production to the Kolla Chapareños. Thus, Kolla coca growers learned from the Cambas the appropriate technique to precipitate the paste from the *aguarrica* (wastes of cocaine and chemicals) after having stomped the coca leaves in kerosene and sulfuric acid.

Today, the Camba organizations in Santa Cruz and the Beni send only lower-echelon members to the Chapare to contact intermediaries (*rescatistas*) to set up the deal with Kollas so that 100–200 kilos of coca paste can be picked up on a certain date. UMOPAR agents are able to spot these Cambas, most of whom are in their early twenties. In the mid-1980s, some Kollas also began to take over coca paste brokerage duties, which had hitherto been carried out only by Cambas.[31] The shift came about when two Kolla women, known as "Chota Rosa" and "Chola Rosa," appeared on the scene.[32] According to the story circulating in the Chapare, both Rosas had the ability to imitate Camba habits. By acting like lowlanders from Santa Cruz and even dressing like them, they were able to pass as lowlanders (Cambas) and thus earn the Camba organizations' confidence. Once arrangements with the Cambas had been made, both women shifted into Kolla attire to confirm their loyalty to the Kolla *cocaleros*, who also trusted them as members of their own culture. In this way, the Rosas became ideal paste brokers facilitating a trade that in essence is interethnic and for which intermediaries are essential. Unfortunately for the Rosas, they have been displaced as the primary brokers in the region by Chichin, king of Isinuta (named after the small village where he operates).[33] The career of the two Rosas has been eclipsed largely because Isinuta became one of the hottest spots for the collection of coca paste in 1990.[34]

When I toured the most active sector for the cocaine paste trade (known as the red area) in October 1990, Camba dealers were still around, and *walkitalkeros*[35] were active in the villages of Eterazama and Isinuta providing their employers with a description of all strangers entering the area. Leaning over their bicycles pretending to change a tire or lounging by the river in an attempt to mask their purpose, the *walkitalkeros* often neglected to conceal the radio antennae protruding from their backs, making their mission more conspicuous than they expected.

On my October 1990 tour of Eterazama, San Gabriel, and Isinuta, a group of Cambas spotted us and jumped out of a parked truck to disappear behind village hovels. These Cambas were young, barely above twenty, and poorly dressed. According to UMOPAR agents, they arrange for coca paste deliveries but move in and out of their operation areas to avoid contact with the UMOPAR as much as possible. "There goes a new line," commented NAU bodyguard Gustavo Araujo in reference to five short men who sneaked away like a school of fish when they saw us coming on the main street of San Gabriel. A "new line" means a new organization, many of which are easily spotted because of the *walkitalkeros*.[36]

Cambas maintain control of the drug trade in the Chapare through a vast information network. To anticipate raids against their laboratories and airstrips, they deploy informers throughout the Chapare region. One NAU official maintains that in Chimoré, drug dealers have set up an observation post at a hotel[37] a few blocks away from the DEA/UMOPAR compound to warn of possible raids on their offices and installations.[38] Prostitutes often gather data from their UMOPAR customers to update the traffickers about every move enforcers plan to make,[39] and in the Chapare, intelligence cannot be separated from the private lives of police officers. For example, Colonel Nicolas Anaya, commander of the UMOPAR in Chimoré during the period of late 1987 to early 1988, developed close relations with a Camba lawyer named Emma Zalarza. Zalarza, a drug dealer herself, was the sister of a top trafficker from Santa Cruz, and it is assumed she conveyed valuable information to him about Leopardo activities.[40] Witnesses add to this account that the woman often dined with her lover at the officers' club at the Chapare's main outpost in Chimoré, and on such occasions, they shared a table with officers from the DEA and the special forces.[41] Zalarza did not confine herself to gathering information by listening to conversations but also discussed her own ideas about how to deal with drug trafficking. The Cambas' ability to stay out of trouble makes it easy and safe for them to establish relations with key figures in the Chapare.

6. THE NEW MODE OF EXCHANGE

Since 1987, traffickers have refused to purchase raw leaf and buy only coca paste from the peasants in the Chapare. Besides transferring from traffickers to peasants the risks and burden of smuggling the necessary materials and utensils, this new method of operation turns growers into accomplices. In this way, the Cambas neutralize any hostility from the peasant unions, because the growers' interests are now tied to those of the Cambas. This new strategy of delegating the first steps of the cocaine trade to the Kollas also allows the Cambas to reduce the size of their networks, which makes them more simple to organize and, consequently, more efficient. In a congressional report, former Bolivian congressman and presidential candidate Roger Cortez called this new mode of production "decentralization."[42] Cortez claimed that by dispersing the illicit manufacturing of coca paste among the population at large, the now enormous number of transgressors of the Bolivian criminal law renders sustained enforcement virtually impossible.

The international drug traffic produces periodical ups and downs in the coca/cocaine business in the Chapare. Antidrug policing efforts can bring the business to a halt and thus cause a collapse in the price of coca/

cocaine for want of purchasers. In February and May 1990, the price of a load of coca[43] fell for stretches of about a week from 150 bolivianos to 10. Subsequently, in only two days, the value of coca skyrocketed. The price surpassed 100 bolivianos in the red area and 120 in Villanueva,[44] and the mark of 160 bolivianos was reached in Eterazama.[45] The vagaries of the market push peasants to increase their participation in coca production and paste manufacturing.

In Bolivia, the new geography of the coca/cocaine business has brought about a new distribution of profits. Although the largest earnings are still being made by the Camba organizations in Santa Cruz and the Beni, a portion of the profits remains with a minority in the Chapare. This minority consists largely of brokers who invest their money in the city of Cochabamba; the vast majority of the Kollas who grow coca in the region remain in poverty.[46]

These changes have also either given birth to or expanded already existing financial institutions. Since the mid-1980s, financiers have been operating in Cochabamba through several financial institutions, including Finsa, Oscobol, and Vial. In 1990 Finsa, allegedly owned by Bismark Barrientos, known as a top trafficker, began to take one-year deposits in U.S. dollars at an annual interest rate of 60 percent. These extremely high interest payments, half of which are paid in advance to the depositors, demonstrate the existing link between the institution and the drug trade, as no other business in Bolivia earns enough to explain such a high rate of return. In 1990, a journalist from Santa Cruz was stabbed almost to death when he tried to investigate Finsa's activities.

7. THE EFFECT OF THE TRANSFORMATION ON KOLLAS

Two broad groups of Kolla producers involved in the Chapare coca/cocaine economy can be delineated: peasants who settled in the Chapare largely in the 1950s and 1960s as part of a government colonization plan implemented jointly with the agrarian reform of 1953; the old-time Chapareños; and recent Kolla migrants who have been both pushed and drawn into the area by ecological disasters and massive unemployment in the highlands, increasing landlessness, and the promise of cash via the cocaine market. These groups have different opinions about cocaine.

The old-time Chapareño Kollas consider the production of coca paste an undesirable response to the cyclical drop in the market value of the coca leaf and the permanent pressure exerted upon them by the traffickers. Although many of these Chapareños are reluctant to join the cocaine trade, they wind up doing so because the coca market can no longer sustain them. In contrast, the recent Kolla migrants have responded to the manufacturing of semirefined cocaine as a more or less natural solution to their inability to make a living in their home regions. Although the earlier Kolla peasant settlers moved into the Chapare with their families,[47] these newcomers are young laborers devoted to the exclusive cultivation of coca because of their immediate need for cash.

With the coca market depressed because of the current drug enforcement policy, with Cambas paying cash on delivery, and with no subsistence crops and thus a total dependency on the cash market, the newcomers turn a large portion of their coca harvests into coca paste. This tack entails monocropping and shifting to cash dependency which means abandoning the traditional indigenous barter economy of the highlands. Because moving to the Chapare to make money rapidly from the cocaine trade is a haphazard and risky venture, families do not usually join in the migration,[48] and Bolivian expert Allyn Stearman recalls having visited areas near Chimoré where there were only men.[49] After selling their own stomped paste, many of these men return to their highland homes only to return to the Chapare a few months later to obtain more cash from coca paste.[50] This pattern is becoming the contemporary migration pattern.

In contrast, the old-time Chapareños long ago developed a subsistence mode of production that is viable for family sustenance. They supplement their coca crops with yucca, rice, citrus fruits, bananas, and other sources of nourishment, and their Chapare is an area where fishing and hunting complement their crops and allow them to enjoy the natural setting. Chapareños who relish this way of life resent the changes introduced by the newcomers' coca monocropping and use of chemicals to make paste for immediate cash. These old settlers claim that the newcomers are not attached to the land, that they exploit it "ruthlessly, like the mines they left in the highlands," and that they will abandon it once it has been rendered sterile.[51]

The old-time Chapareños also view the newcomers' aggressive marketing policies as a threat to their own traditional place in the coca trade and to their cultural and physical environment. "Trees are being felled everywhere and invariably replaced by coca plantations," protests one Chapareño, and indeed, in October 1990, vast sectors of the Chapare forest were slashed and burned, and smoke columns could be seen everywhere. In addition, new settlers are bribing state colonization officials to demarcate new plots in such a way that they often overlap previous land concessions, which results in frequent scuffles. The lack of administrative authorities to settle conflicts in the area forces the old settlers to surrender their disputed land tamely or face violent assaults from the recent migrants.[52]

Growing coca strongly attracts newcomers because it requires less work and demands far less investment than any other agricultural production. But this mode is at variance with the older Chapareños' conception of the place coca has in their economy. To plant subsistence crops and some coca and stomp paste for the family's sustenance is admissible. Associating with Cambas and sowing only coca to make an immediate profit, regardless of the consequences, is unacceptable.

The degradation of the Chapare as a result of the cocaine boom is not just a matter of older Chapareños' opinion, as the present coca/cocaine economy has had catastrophic effects on the environment. Sulfuric acid utilized in making the basic paste is contaminating the soil, and the rivers are becoming polluted and barren of fish.[53] One native Chapareño I met in a bar in the port of San Francisco exhibited an infected elbow. It had become infected a week earlier when he bathed in the San Francisco River, much as he had done since his childhood. The old-timers feel that the cocaine trade is distorting their culture, turning their children into addicts, breaking family ties, and destroying their lives.

In September 1989, I met Anacleto, a forty-seven-year-old Chapareño who blamed the newcomers for the destruction of his family. His twenty-two-year-old son worked for one of the newcomers. He was paid with *pitucos* and, to ensure his continued labor, was made to chew coca with the toxic leftovers of sulfuric acid and kerosene used in coca paste manufacturing. Anacleto's son had become a heavy addict. Some years earlier, a newcomer seduced Anacleto's wife by forcing her to smoke cocaine paste. Anacleto argued that there is no way a woman can resist a man that makes her smoke paste. The newcomer killed her some time later, Anacleto related, when she grew dependent on him for more paste.[54]

Anacleto also complained of having been compelled to join one of the local peasant unions. Their leaders, he claimed, are corrupt and subordinate the affiliates to their own illicit business, and the case of Julio Rocha supports that assertion. Rocha is a renowned leader who has headed several uprisings in the Chapare, including the invasion of Villa Tunari's UMOPAR outpost on June 27, 1988.[55] Rocha, as even his own union comrades suspect,[56] owns several plots in the Chapare and employs peasants to make coca paste. Anibal Aguilar, when under-secretary of alternative development in the Paz-Estenssoro administration, formally accused Rocha of being involved in dealings with traffickers' organizations,[57] and there was more against Rocha than Aguilar's indictment. Enrique Valverde, the head of the NAU in Cochabamba until 1990, had Rocha fly with him and UMOPAR personnel on a helicopter tour over the Chapare jungle. When the enforcement party detected five peasants stomping coca paste, the pilot made a quick landing downwind from the stompers, which enabled Valverde and two Leopardos to slip briskly through the bush to surround and arrest them. Questioned on the spot by Valverde, the detainees asserted that the coca paste belonged to the owner of the plots where they were stomping and that the proprietor was among Valverde's team and was standing in front of them. That man was Julio Rocha.[58]

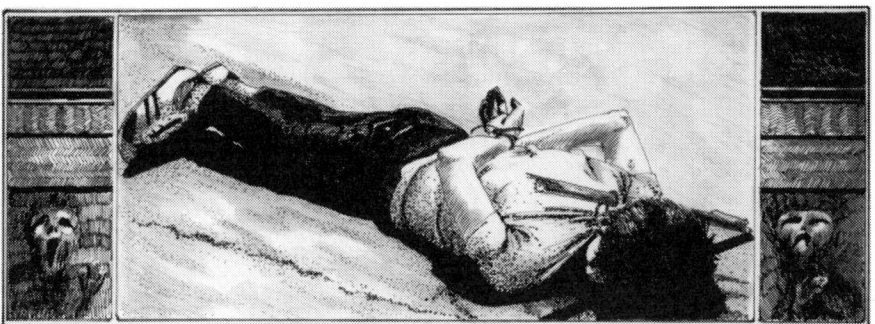

Old-time Chapareños often share Anacleto's sense of impotence concerning the changes taking place in the Chapare. Becoming entangled in the present coca/cocaine economy is not only increasingly indispensable for financial reasons but also increasingly unsafe. Victor, for example, gave up the local leadership of the Chapare Tropical union in San Francisco and is no longer in the transport business with his small boat. To ferry drugs in the Chapare and the Beni means trouble—the bodies of carriers found floating in the river testify to the danger involved.[59] Nobody in the transport business can evade carrying coca paste. If a carrier refuses to transport coca paste upriver when it is his turn to do so, he faces reprisals from the transporters' unions. Like every boat owner, Victor was forced to take whatever merchandise was assigned to him, and all too often, the pouches he transported contained paste destined for the northern territory of Isiboro Secure, where there are numerous airstrips. Entanglement with the police or naval patrols was inevitable, and the UMOPAR or the navy would board his boat to levy a "tax" on the coca paste he carried. Oftentimes, such journeys wind up in skirmishes with the authorities when the armed Camba passengers try to keep the authorities from boarding a boat.

8. CONCLUSIONS

In the next chapter, I describe the enforcement policy and explain its failure to cope with the top traffickers. From this first chapter and the next two, it will be obvious that the war on drugs contributes to the current situation. Enforcement campaigns to capture the head traffickers in the 1980s failed, and the trafficking networks remain intact. U.S. efforts to overcome the weaknesses of local enforcement by providing support in the field have also proved inefficient, as the participation of DEA agents in the field in joint efforts with the UMOPAR has not improved everyday enforcement. The inability to control traffic at the top has spawned a shift in the policy to persecution of the small producers in the Chapare. The UMOPAR has elected to exact "taxes" on stompers or to arrest them when that is not feasible. This strategy involves less risk than confronting traffickers' bodyguards and ensures periodic drug seizures and arrests, which can be cited as a sign of an enforcement "breakthrough." Statistics can thus satisfy the expectations of the U.S. agencies concerned with drug enforcement.[60]

Although the U.S.-Bolivian official approach serves the purpose of lowering the price of raw coca by partially deterring its demand, the shortcomings of this strategy are evident. The main traffickers remain in business, and the exporting of cocaine hydrochloride continues. There is still a permanent demand for coca paste—and no other alternative for the landless and unemployed Kollas. So far, the repression campaign has dispersed coca manufacturing among a larger segment of the population and resulted in an inescapable vicious circle. As enforcement lowers the price of raw coca, more Bolivians are forced to engage in the drug trade. As U.S. and Bolivian agents' compounds are surrounded by more peasants engaging in the trade, enforcement is impeded.

NOTES

1. January 19, 1990, issue.

2. It was the morning of Wednesday, January 16, 1990. The same day, the La Paz newspaper *El Pais* carried a picture of the Leopardos burning a ton of coca. It did not mention senators from the United States, but it did mention congressmen (see unofficial translation of report submitted by the Subcommittee on Information, Justice and Agriculture, presided over by John Conyers, in La Paz newspaper *Ultima Hora*, August 30, 1990).

3. James A. Inciardi, *The War on Drugs: Heroin, Cocaine, Crime, and Public Policy* (Mountain View, Calif.: Mayfield Publishing Company, 1984), p. 178.

4. Another example of oversimplifying the Bolivian picture is supplied by Scott MacDonald, who claims that the 1952 revolution that displaced General Hugo Ballivián's regime was largely responsible for the development of a cocaine oligarchy in Bolivia. MacDonald's main argument is that because military authority was thus weakened, parts of the country acquired an excessive autonomy that led to the formation of drug-run regions (see Scott B. MacDonald, *Mountain High, White Avalanche: Cocaine and Power in the Andean States and Panama*, Washington Papers no. 137 [New York: Praeger, 1989], p. 68). Two essential points are missed by MacDonald. First, regional cultures have always been dominant in Bolivia; if anything, the revolution of 1952 attempted to create a national movement to envelop regional diversity. Second, in Bolivia, the drug oligarchies developed much later, during two military dictatorships: It was during General Hugo Banzer-

Suarez's rule (1971-1978), that unsuccessful cotton growers from Santa Cruz moved into the Chapare for raw substances to develop a cocaine industry, and in the early 1980s, the cocaine business gained its present size when General Luis Garcia-Meza and his minister of the interior, Colonel Luis Arce-Gomez, set up the famous Bolivian "cocaine dictatorship." Both generals distinguished themselves, not for encouraging regional autonomy, but by their attempt to exercise concentrated power.

5. See Anibal Aguilar-Gomez (under-secretary for crop substitution during the Paz-Estenssoro administration), "El impacto desestructurador del capital paralelo sobre la economia campesina," *Procampo*, November 1987.

6. Juan Jose Castro and Walter Gomez, "Crisis economica y perspectivas de la democracia," in *Democracia a la deriva: Dilemas de la participación y concertación social en Bolivia* (La Paz: PNUD, CLACSO, CERES, 1987), p. 177.

7. Crandon defines Ayllu as an "extended kinship organization that involves reciprocal obligations, especially ayni, and mutual support" (Libbet Crandon, *From the Fat of Our Souls* [Berkeley and Los Angeles: University of California Press, 1991], p. 247).

8. Some observers attribute the fiasco to the attempt to make up for the forgone profits by selling shorter-strand cotton, which was rejected by European purchasers. This version is espoused by Enrique Valverde, chief of the NAU in Cochabamba until 1990.

9. Susan Eckstein, "Transformation of a Revolution from Below: Bolivia and International Capitalism," *Comparative Studies in Society and History* 25 (1983), p. 205.

10. Allyn MacLean Stearman underlines the importance of the cocaine market in this locality since the mid-1970s (*Camba and Kolla: Migration and Development in Santa Cruz, Bolivia* [Orlando: University of Central Florida Press, 1985], p. 133). The same information was given to me in an interview with Enrique Valverde, May 30, 1990.

11. Gonzalo Flores and José Blanes, *Donde va el Chapare?* (Cochabamba: Centro de Estudios de la Realidad Economica y Social, 1984), p. 140.

12. See the La Paz archbishop's exhortation to the government for aid to peasants (Msgr. Luis Sainz, *Presencia*, March 3, 1990). See also *Presencia*, April 13, 1990.

13. See, for example, Colin Sage, "Drugs and Economic Development in Latin America: A Study in the Political Bolivian Economy of Cocaine in Bolivia," in *Corruption, Development, and Inequality*, ed. Peter M. Ward (London and New York: Routledge, 1989), p. 44.

14. Anthony Henman, "Cocaine Futures," in *Big Deal: The Politics of the Illicit Drugs Business*, ed. Anthony Henman, Roger Lewis, and Tim Malyon (London and Sydney: Pluto Press, 1985), p. 152; Kevin Healy, "The Boom Within the Crisis: Some Recent Effects of Foreign Cocaine Markets on Bolivian Rural Society and Economy," in *Coca and Cocaine: Effects on People and Policy in Latin America*, ed. Deborah Paccini and Christine Franquemont, Cultural Survival Report, Latin American Studies Program (Ithaca, N.Y.: Cornell University, 1985), p. 126; and Healy, "Coca, the State, and Peasantry in Bolivia, 1982-1988," *Journal of Interamerican Studies and World Affairs* 30:2-3 (Summer/Fall 1988), p. 121.

15. Henman, "Cocaine Futures," p. 149.
16. See Chapter 2, section 6.
17. See Jo Ann Kawell, "The Addict Economies," *NACLA* 22:6 (March 1989), pp. 33–38. For the role some of these materials play in coca paste manufacturing, see the Introduction to this book.
18. Each village has its own peasants' union, and in the Chapare, there are 170 such unions grouped in twenty-one *centrales* (main unions) (see Bernard Louis Delaine, *Coca Farming in the Chapare: A Form of Collective Innovation* [Ph.D. dissertation, Saint Louis University; Ann Arbor, Mich.: University Microfilms International, 1990], p. 57).
19. Interview with Enrique Valverde, Villa Tunari, October 5, 1990.
20. Montaño became a staunch advocate of spending resources in the valleys and highlands to attract their original inhabitants back. In 1987, Montaño resigned when he opposed Paz-Estenssoro's program for "alternative development" and Anibal Aguilar-Gomez, the under-secretary of alternative development, insisted on spending most of the funds available in the Chapare (interview with an engineer from DIRECO, Chapare, May 1990).
21. Interview with Montaño, La Paz, May 21, 1990.
22. The Plan Trienal of 1986 pursued the same goals as the U.S.-Bolivian Operation Blast Furnace: to dissuade peasants from growing coca by dumping the price of the leaf below costs (see José Antonio Quiroga, "Paradojas de una responsabilidad compartida," *Nueva Sociedad* [Caracas], no. 102 [July-August 1989], p. 169). The same goal was made explicit in the Cartagena Accord signed by Presidents Bush, Virgilio Barco of Colombia, Alan Garcia of Peru, and Paz-Zamora in February 1990.
23. There are times when the price is so low that even dealing in coca paste becomes inviable. In February and May 1990, for instance, the value of coca collapsed from 150 bolivianos a load to 10 or 12. However, these periods have not lasted more than a few weeks. I deal with this issue in Chapter 4, section 3.
24. Interview with Enrique Valverde, September 16, 1989, and interviews with Cochabamba research institution CIDRE physician Mario Argandoña, January 15, 1990, and sociologist Julio Alem, May 27, 1990.
25. The NAU (Narcotics Assistance Unit) is under the jurisdiction of the INM (International Narcotic Matters) based in Washington, D.C. The main responsibilities of the NAU consist of funding crop substitution programs and designing strategies to obtain the contribution of the host countries. Additionally, the NAU/INM combination administers funds for enforcement, and in Bolivia, this role has become prominent (see Ethan A. Nadelman, "Cops Across Borders: Transnational Crime and International Law Enforcement" [Ph.D. dissertation, Harvard University, Political Science Department, June 1987], p. 258).
26. Enrique Valverde, Villa Tunari, May 30, 1990.
27. Interview with former presidential candidate and congressman Roger Cortez, La Paz, January 9, 1990.
28. Interviews with Enrique Valverde, Villa Tunari, May 30, 1990, and Roger Cortez, La Paz, January 9, 1990.

29. UMOPAR is short for Unidad Mobil de Patrullaje Rural (Mobile Unit of Rural Patrol). Members of this unit are also called Leopardos (see Chapter 2, sections 1 and 3).

30. See Chapter 2, section 1.

31. See what is known as the "Conyers' Commission Report" (*Ultima Hora*, August 30, 1990), John Conyers being the chairman of the Subcommittee for Information of Government, Justice and Agriculture of the U.S. on Bolivia, Peru and Colombia. For the official version, see U.S. Congress, Committee on Government Operations, Subcommittee for Information of Government, Justice and Agriculture, "Thirty-Eighth Report: United States Anti-Narcotics Activities in the Andean Region" (Washington, D.C., November 1990).

32. In local parlance, "Chola" stands for Kolla woman and "Chota" for a Camba female, and it is almost impossible to know who is who when the Chola dresses like the Chota or the Chota is disguised as a Chola (Enrique Valverde, Chapare, October 5, 1990). Ex–Foreign Affairs Minister Bedregal-Gutierrez claims that Chola Rosa's real name is Rosa Romero de Húmerez (see Guillermo Bedregal-Gutierrez and Ruddy Viscarra-Pando, *La lucha boliviana contra el narcotrafico* [La Paz: Los Amigos del Libro, 1989], p. 167).

33. Interview with La Paz *Ultima Hora* journalist and writer José Antonio Quiroga, Santa Cruz, La Paz, September 30, 1990.

34. See Chapter 2, section 9.

35. Name derived from walkie talkie; *walkitalkeros* are Chapareños whose mission is to forewarn the Cambas about possible danger, especially from the UMOPAR or the DEA.

36. Interview with Gustavo Araujo, a Paraguayan NAU employee, Chimoré, May 28, 1990.

37. The UMOPAR driver, whom I asked for details, thought it was the Hotel Napoles.

38. Chapare, January 16, 1990.

39. Interview with Enrique Valverde, Cochabamba, January 14, 1990.

40. This story was confirmed by everyone who served in that outpost at the time, and it coincides with the promiscuity referred to in the Bolivian version of the Conyers' report (*Ultima Hora*) August 30, 1990). *Ultima Hora* quotes Congressman Conyers, who visited the Chapare as the head of an investigative commission of the U.S. House of Representatives, as saying that the Chimoré barracks were a mess, and that officers' lovers and even prostitutes walked in and out of the site at will.

41. Interviews with Enrique Valverde, May 26, 1990, and Gustavo Araujo, May 28, 1990.

42. "Informe Parlamentario del Caso Huanchaca" (unpublished 1986), p. 27.

43. A load of coca (*carga*) is equal to 45 kilos (100 pounds).

44. Villanueva's coca is reportedly new. Experts in the region had considered this area as one in which eradication efforts had succeeded.

45. Among other sources, a conversation with two men who work for Eudoro Barrientos, a conspicuous and controversial peasant union leader, Villanueva, May 28, 1990.

46. According to José Blanes, Fernando Calderón, et al. in *Tras nuevas raices: Migraciones internas y colonizacion en Bolivia* (La Paz: Proyecto Politico de Poblacion, Ministerio de Planeamiento, n.d.), 78 percent of the Chapare settlers own only one plot of land (*parcela*), but in Yapacani, a Santa Cruz region that borders on the Chapare, only 49 percent own only one plot (p. 117). A plot's size varies between 1 and 40 hectares, and the cropping surface is greatly reduced because of a lack of machinery to fill in the swamps or cut down the dense forest (p. 118).

47. See Xavier Albó, Kitula Liberman, et al., *Para comprender las culturas rurales en Bolivia* (La Paz: Ministerio de Educacion y Cultura, 1989), p. 190.

48. As hazards, Michael Painter cites regional diseases, poor diet, and medical problems as well as police repression and traffickers' reprisals ("Institutional Analysis of the Chapare Regional Development Project" [Institute for Development Anthropology, Clark University, Worcester, Massachusetts, and Institute for Development Anthropology, Binghamton, New York, 1990], p. 42).

49. Conversation with Allyn Stearman in the city of Cochabamba, May 27, 1990.

50. Ibid.

51. Flores y Blanes, *Donde va el Chapare?* p. 140.

52. Interviews in the Chapare with Enrique Valverde, January 17, 1990, and Leopardo Captain Mario Ayala, May 29, 1990.

53. See Delaine, *Coca Farming in the Chapare*, p. 42.

54. Interview in San Miguel, Chapare, September 16, 1989.

55. Interview with journalist Elva Morales, Cochabamba, January 15, 1990. For the Villa Tunari incident, see Chapter 2, section 5.

56. Interview with COB (Bolivian Workers' Corporation) leader Secundino Montevilla at the COB's offices in La Paz on September 1, 1989. Julio Rocha, Felipe Tapia, and a third union official allegedly are involved in paste manufacturing.

57. Interview with Secundino Montevilla, La Paz, January 10, 1990.

58. Interview with Enrique Valverde in the Chapare, September 15, 1990.

59. Interview in the Chapare port of San Francisco with a local union leader, Victor, January 16, 1990.

60. Methods used by enforcement agencies to assess their achievements are a source of concern for the U.S. Congress Committee on Government Operations. The use of "microlevel indicators" such as "arrests" and "seizures" is one disputable aspect of these assessments (see U.S. Congress, Committee on Government Operations, Thirty-Eighth Report: United States Anti-Narcotics Activities in the Andean Region" [Washington, D.C., August 30, 1990], p. 30. See also, Jose Mirtembaum, anthropologist and ex-adviser to the COB, "Frente a la militarización consideramos la legalización" [Unpublished paper, 1990], and Chapter 5, section 2).

2

Joint U.S.-Bolivian Enforcement and Eradication

> *I do not know where the ambassador may have gotten the information from. Bolivia has proven to be the first country in fighting narco-traffic in Latin America and has beaten all records of efficiency in that terrain.*
> —President Paz Zamora, in response to public complaints from U.S. Ambassador Robert Gelbard; *La Razon* (La Paz), September 27, 1990

1. HOW TO PROTECT DEMOCRACY: RECIPES FROM THE UNITED STATES

During his presidency of Bolivia from 1982 to 1985, Hernan Siles-Suazo was pressured by the United States to adopt drastic measures to curb the cocaine traffic and substantially bring down coca production.[1] The scope and complexity of the Bolivian cocaine economy were the principal reasons why Siles did not initially give in to the U.S. pressure. As a man of vast political experience, and as the first popularly elected president in the country in eighteen years, Siles considered a major repressive campaign against the drug business to be a dangerous approach. The involvement of highly ranked military and police officers in the drug trade during the Garcia-Meza regime, and the inability of the democratic institutions to control the armed forces, were well known in Bolivia.[2]

Nevertheless, in August 1983, as pressure from the U.S. Embassy continued, the Bolivian government agreed to eradicate 4,000 hectares of coca. This task would be carried out by the Bolivian state's technical office,

DIRECO,[3] and policed by the UMOPAR (Mobile Unit of Rural Patrol), whose members are commonly known as Leopardos. The UMOPAR is a special police unit devised to enforce drug laws in the jungle, cocaine manufacturing and trafficking in particular. This new special police branch is considered a "paramilitary group" by many political observers, including officials in the U.S. State Department.[4] Devised as an elite force, the 580 Leopardos[5] are chosen from among the most able police officers to receive special training by U.S. personnel. As an acknowledgment by the U.S. government of their cooperation, each Leopardo receives from the Narcotics Assistance Unit (NAU)[6] a monthly $50 bonus.[7]

The UMOPAR, however, has not always devoted all its efforts to policing infringements of antidrug laws. On June 30, 1984, members of this corps joined army personnel to stage Bolivia's 251st armed coup,[8] a coup led by German Linares, Carlos Barriga, and Julio Diaz-Vargas,[9] three high-ranking Leopardo officers who were allegedly involved in drug trafficking. As part of the plot, the Leopardo second in command, Linares, abducted Siles[10] with the support of Lieutenant Colonel Anaya, Vice-President Jaime Paz-Zamora's army aide. Meanwhile, UMOPAR Captain Ciro Gigena[11] took over the building of the Ministry of the Interior to control all police forces in the country.[12] Opposition to the mutiny by a large sector of the army enabled Siles to negotiate his way out of captivity, but at the cost of facilitating the plotters' escape by having them driven in his own car into exile at the Argentinean Embassy.[13]

Although the coup failed and thus did not establish a replica of the 1980–1981 cocaine dictatorship of Garcia-Meza, it clearly conveyed how deeply embedded the drug trade is in Bolivian political life. It also exposed the threat that the young Leopardo antidrug unit could pose to the democratic experiment should the army support a Leopardo officers' attempt to overthrow the government, or even simply refuse to interfere. When the civilian government enjoys minimal consensus, a combination of army and police is improbable because interforce rivalries get in the way.[14] However, in times of crisis, the threat of such an alliance becomes substantial as general discontent encourages a coalition of this sort, no matter how ephemeral. A lack of confidence in the government, however passing, can easily tempt the UMOPAR and the army to reach a momentary agreement conducive to a takeover.[15] Bolivia's next constitutional president, Victor Paz-Estenssoro, was aware of the danger of a new attempt to take over the government and thus felt compelled to reinstate Linares, one of the main rebel officers. In May 1990, Barriga was posted in Trinidad to command the UMOPAR units operating in the northern Amazon region of the Beni.[16] In January 1990, back on duty, Diaz-Vargas was in the middle of a mess and charged with extorting money from an alleged cocaine trafficker whom he illegally allowed to escape.[17] Such events reveal the fragility of the democratic experiment and the government's need to compromise with the powerful drug interests in order to survive at all.

U.S. policymakers at the time did not seem to be aware of the fragility of the new Bolivian democracy. Thus, the institutional weakness of Bolivia depicted by Siles's June 30 abduction did not deter U.S. Senator Paula Hawkins, member of the Senate's Subcommittee on Drug Abuse and Narcotics and a close friend of President Reagan,[18] from complaining about the Bolivian government. Hawkins claimed that the country's administration was neglecting its duty to stop the cocaine trade, and on a visit to La Paz on July 8, shortly after Siles's release, she warned that the United States would withhold $58 million for aid unless strong steps were taken against the drug business.[19] Seemingly ignorant of the recent activities of UMOPAR and army officers, the U.S. senator took the opportunity to add that the cocaine traffic was a serious menace to democratic institutions.

In response to Hawkins's threat, the Siles administration decided to convey a different image to the United States by placing the Chapare under military control.[20] A joint antidrug operation was thus staged with 1,500 army troops and UMOPAR units in Bolivia's largest coca growing region on the eastern side of the Andes. U.S. Ambassador Edwin Corr welcomed the initiative and denying any relationship to U.S. pressure, reconfirmed that the $58 million in aid would be invested in Bolivia.[21]

The Chapare operation resulted in the destruction of several million dollars worth of coca paste, the confiscation of a few aircraft and arms, and the arrest of a number of small cocaine paste manufacturers and brokers. Having been informed of the operation well ahead of time, the major traffickers had comfortably escaped by the time the troops stormed the region.[22] Arrested were only a few small dealers and about fifty stompers. The operation brought about a great deal of unrest among the peasants, who feared their coca crops would be the army's next target. Peasant unions mobilized 5,000 growers on October 29 and blockaded the roads in the Chapare, which hindered surface communication between the country's tropical eastern plains and the western highlands. The siege was lifted only when the government promised the peasants that their coca crops would not be destroyed. To ensure their means of livelihood, the growers subsequently went on a hunger strike, demanding the withdrawal of troops and the granting of a license to continue cultivating and marketing coca. As a result, the administration allowed growers to take out of the Chapare 11 kilos of coca each week for each peasant family's consumption. Furthermore, individual growers could legally sell an unlimited amount of coca to the state and deposit it in the state's leaf dumps. The military campaign did not prevent further large-scale cocaine business, and cocaine production and traffic soon regained their former size. But this experience did not lead the U.S. administration to question the original drug war approach, and further repressive campaigns continue to be perceived as the proper strategy to follow to reduce the flow of cocaine from Bolivia.

2. OPERATION BLAST FURNACE

President Reagan's declaration that drug trafficking was a threat to the U.S. national security, issued in a secret directive on April 8, 1986,[23] had direct repercussions on the Bolivian war on drugs. The institutional gravity revealed by the U.S. president's order set the scenario for a new, large militarized enforcement campaign in Bolivia. From April 26 to May 6 of that year, Leopardos and U.S. military forces were deployed in joint maneuvers in the departments of Santa Cruz and Cochabamba in preparation for the joint U.S.-Bolivian Operation Blast Furnace, and after six months of planning, the operation was launched on July 18, 1986. The legitimacy of the U.S. intervention was formally grounded by the Reagan administration in a request from the Bolivian executive branch and the Lara Bonilla Treaty, an agreement that was only ratified by the Bolivian Congress in May 1990, four years after Operation Blast Furnace took place. As expressed by the U.S. Embassy in Bolivia, the ultimate goal of the joint operation was to lower the market price of coca leaf. In the belief that destroying cocaine laboratories would reduce the demand for raw coca,[24] 160 U.S. military troops and UMOPAR units were transported into the Beni, the Chapare, and Santa Cruz on six U.S. Black Hawk helicopters, and an airlift was set up between La Paz and Trinidad where the operation's headquarters were installed.

Operation Blast Furnace did not succeed. No major drug dealer was arrested, and large laboratories were found dismantled. The operating forces had to make do with destroying coca paste pits, which can be dug in a few hours. Military experts attribute the failure of what has been properly labeled as the "Americanization" of enforcement[25] to three factors. First, leaked data concerning the operation aroused the resistance of local politicians and members of the Congress in particular, who viewed the presence of foreign troops as an unjustifiable intrusion on the part of the United States, an incursion that Congress had not consented to. In accord with local politicians' views, the international press perceived the operation as a U.S. abuse of that country's financial power over the Bolivian government, which undermined the country's institutional life. Second, easy identification of the aircraft employed in the campaign enabled the traffickers to anticipate the move, and third, different conceptions of how to carry out the mission led to rifts among U.S. forces, the DEA, and the Bolivian UMOPAR.[26] Argentinean drug enforcement experts attribute those conflicts to the diverse training of police and military officers, which

affected these forces' methods despite their overlapping duties.[27] A NAU official records that one of the U.S. top army officers connected with Operation Blast Furnace confirmed this opinion by asserting, off the record, that he would vehemently oppose any attempt to stage another such operation. The officer claimed that coordination and cooperation among the participating forces were deplorable.[28]

Although no official sources in the United States would admit that Operation Blast Furnace was a failure, the Reagan administration responded to local public outrage by making the U.S. military presence in Bolivia less conspicuous, and the Bush administration has so far followed suit. The 160 U.S. soldiers who participated in the operation were flown back home and were replaced by a dozen special forces personnel. As I discovered in 1988, on my trip as President Alfonsin's envoy, these soldiers refuse to disclose any information concerning their military condition or what they are up to in Bolivia.[29]

Among Bolivian politicians, the operation is still irksome, and they still consider it an unwarranted intrusion of foreign armed forces made possible by the Paz-Estenssoro administration's compliance with the Reagan administration. The claim entertained by the Bolivian government that Blast Furnace was not a military operation but an enforcement campaign that required no congressional approval did not appease the enraged opposition. Whatever the label, Bolivia had been invaded by foreign troops over which the Paz-Estenssoro government had no control whatsoever.

3. DRUG LAW ENFORCERS IN 1990

In October 1990, a dozen soldiers from the U.S. Army's special forces still remained in the Chapare. Like the U.S. Border Patrol and DEA agents, these soldiers were deployed in the Chapare for three- or four-month periods. Special forces troopers share a barracks compound with the U.S. Border Patrol, the DEA, and the UMOPAR near the village of Chimoré. Their responsibility is no longer in the field,[30] instead, their mission is now confined to training the Leopardos in jungle warfare. The border patrol instructs the local police at customs checkpoints where drugs, chemicals, and manufacturing utensils are being smuggled in and out of the Chapare region, and apart from an intelligence assignment, the DEA also performs an advisory role.

The UMOPAR supreme chief, army General Lucio Añez, has flatly stated that the forty DEA officers deployed in Bolivia since 1988 must limit their task to supplying information and technical advice to Bolivian agencies, but experience indicates that the DEA role has been broader. In practice, they largely command the UMOPAR on assignments when they do not operate on their own. One example of the DEA's independence was displayed on a television show in La Paz on October 1, 1990. On September 22, at 6 P.M., journalists from the "Linea de Fuego" television show in La Paz were intercepted near a burning stomping pit on the road that links Isiboro and Isinuta. Two men, visibly Americans, did not approach the lorry but stayed on the edge of the road speaking English to each other. A third man, with a strong, distinct Mexican accent, respectfully queried the crew and let them go on their way after they had exhibited their credentials. This incident was shown on Bolivian television, and although insignificant in itself, it is only one of many in which the DEA has displayed its operational independence.[31]

The way in which DEA officers carry out their assignments in the field has been questioned by the rest of the U.S. agencies in Bolivia, especially special forces personnel. They claim that once they have fulfilled their task of training UMOPAR officers in jungle warfare, these officers are instructed by the DEA to operate in ways that contradict the special forces' training, which leads to confusion among Bolivian enforcers. It is also claimed that the DEA officers themselves lack preparation and that some of them have taken only a brief survival course before they arrive in Bolivia.[32]

Both the DEA and the border patrol can hardly overcome Bolivia's puzzling situation. Like the U.S. special forces, members of each agency remain in the country for stretches varying between three and four months, which has proved too short to learn enough about the new environment in which they must operate. This deficiency has been noticed by local officers who claim that most of the U.S. agents cannot speak Spanish. Furthermore, the fact that each U.S. team of DEA and border patrol officers is entirely replaced by fresh personnel means the newcomers lack the benefit of past experience.[33]

Drug enforcement in the Bolivian bush often requires the use of helicopters to ferry personnel. In the beginning, the fleet consisted of two Llama helicopters donated by the French government, but they proved highly impractical. Not only were they too small to carry Leopardos, but they were also often inactive because of a lack of spare parts. Bolivia then borrowed eight UH1H helicopters from the United States. Although these helicopters display the Bolivian flag, agreements with the United States require that they not be flown without at least one DEA official on board.

The Bolivian Air Force and Navy play a complementary role in drug law enforcement.[34] The air force has been assigned the duty of ferrying UMOPAR and DEA officers, and according to the U.S. Embassy in La Paz,[35] the air force pilots, called "red devils," are so efficient in managing the Huey helicopters that not a single accident had been reported (this safety record continued until October 1990 and is perhaps still standing). Naval officers and air force pilots are members of the Bolivian special forces, which provide support and technical assistance to jungle-trained UMOPAR and urban antidrug police units.[36] Since early April 1990, the controversial presence of army regiments Ustariz and Barrientos carrying out what the military calls routine drills,[37] has added a new and conflictive ingredient to enforcement in the Chapare.[38]

Until April 1990, the army had no permanent involvement in drug enforcement, having only participated in a few large-scale operations like the April 1982 joint military and police takeover of the Chapare and the militarization of the area in October 1984. Nonetheless, as a consequence of the Cartagena meeting held in February 1990 by Presidents Paz-Zamora, Garcia of Peru, Barco of Colombia, and Bush, the Bolivian government committed itself to having the army engage in drug enforcement on a permanent basis, and this commitment was ratified in Annex 3 signed by Presidents Bush and Paz-Zamora on May 9, 1990, as an addendum to the agreement reached in Cartagena. By mid-May, one light infantry regiment of roughly 800 men was bivouacking in the Chapare, near Chimoré, to enter the war on drugs. Although no active intervention in the drug war had been reported by October, the commander of the brigade, General Victor Vargas, claimed optimistically that the sole presence of his troops was having a strong dissuasive effect on the drug business, and the soldiers also protect peasants against alleged abuses from the UMOPAR and the DEA.[39] As a part of the special forces, the Bolivian Navy's permanent role in drug enforcement consists of watching over ports and boat traffic on the wide Amazon River tributaries in the eastern lowlands. It also ferries personnel on U.S.-made Piranha boats in and out of the northern region of the Beni, large portions of which are inaccessible by land owing to the absence of roads.

The stress on drug enforcement in Bolivia has led to contradictory outcomes. In spite of the importance given by U.S.-Bolivian officials to enforcement, the special body created to carry out the task, the UMOPAR, is underequipped because of interference from rival Bolivian military officers, some of whom believe that the Leopardos are totally corrupt and that, having sold their loyalty to the U.S. Embassy, they cannot be differentiated from the DEA. The commander of the Barrientos Battalion, Colonel Rodriguez, while getting his troops ready for the war on drugs, stated in May 1990 that the task of the military should be to first terminate the UMOPAR and then carry out the assignment against drug manufacturers and dealers.[40]

To retain its traditional clout, the army has induced the government and the U.S. Embassy to make sure the UMOPAR resources remain at a level below that of the army's resources. Hence, the UMOPAR receives privileged training from the DEA, the special forces, and the border patrol, but its operating capacity has been deliberately thwarted. Old-model carbines and precarious communications equipment generate major difficulties in the execution of UMOPAR assignments. Patrols are often isolated, as UMOPAR Major Julio Arana explained to me in September 1989 at the Chapare outpost of Villa Tunari, and the lack of modern radio equipment impedes efficient operations against drug traffickers in the mountainous jungle areas of the Chapare and the high rain forest in the Beni, northern Santa Cruz, and Pando. The radio equipment—one UMOPAR captain explained[41]—is obsolete,[42] and ammunition for practice is very scanty and so are spare magazines.

Paz-Zamora's interior minister, Guillermo Capobianco, witnessed personally the jammed carbines, the lack of ammunition, and the difficult conditions in which the UMOPAR were living in the Chapare.[43] Few UMOPAR personnel, the minister acknowledged, had mattresses to sleep on,[44] and even though the belief that the "druggies" (*pichicateros*) are equipped with sophisticated gear is incorrect, the UMOPAR is easily outgunned by their Uzis and MAC 10s. The most demoralizing issue according to one UMOPAR officer is that the army is getting new equipment from the United States. "One wonders who does General Añez stand by; one would bet it is the army."[45]

According to some observers, the UMOPAR is not only under-equipped but most of its agents are virtually defenseless. Most of the 580 members of the well-trained force[46] have taken the Garras del Valor course, a course founded by Yellman, the highly respected NAU head in La Paz in 1988, and designed by the DEA to train the UMOPAR in jungle survival and warfare. At first, the course was taught by the U.S. special forces in Bolivia, but over time, UMOPAR officers have gradually replaced their U.S. instructors, and today, the course is entirely taught by Bolivian personnel under U.S. special forces' supervision. The U.S. Embassy's idea is to keep the UMOPAR as a small, elite force,[47] but until August 1990, when most of the force was supplied with U.S. modern M16 assault rifles,[48] only 50 officers had been equipped with modern weaponry. In January 1990, traffickers ambushed a UMOPAR patrol searching for cocaine hydrochloride in the region of Isiboro Secure, killing one Leopardo outright and severely wounding another. The chief of police of Cochabamba, Colonel Eddy Villaroel, reacted immediately to the episode and openly requested the withdrawal of the UMOPAR from active duty in the Chapare because the inadequacy of its equipment was making their task far too risky.[49]

4. THE DRUG ENFORCEMENT AGENCY

The reputation of the UMOPAR and the DEA agents in Bolivia is controversial. The inhabitants of the Beni, the Chapare, and the Yungas charge the UMOPAR with harassment and pillage performed with the support of the DEA.[50] This view, repeatedly espoused by coca growers, has received support from the Bolivian Senate[51] and sectors of the Catholic church, and citizens of the Beni, including farmers and businesspeople, issued a strong condemnation against UMOPAR procedures, claiming they imposed a serious risk upon the innocent inhabitants of the region.[52] President Paz-Zamora's under-secretary of social defense, Gonzalo Torrico, responded by blaming the traffickers for what he deemed were slanderous charges against the special police force,⁵³ but those allegations were discredited by his boss, Guillermo Capobianco. Minister of the Interior Capobianco admitted that the UMOPAR had perpetrated abuses against the populace in the Chapare and the Beni, and he addressed the UMOPAR personnel in the Chapare, "recommending more respect for civilians" given the well-grounded accusations that the force had been abusing women and illegally "hindering trade."⁵⁴ In October 1990, Bolivian Congressman Julio Mantilla-Cuellar publicly declared that the UMOPAR had been exacting money from coca growers in the Yungas. Mantilla formally asked the Ministry of the Interior to inform the Chamber of Deputies about reported cases of torture and property invasion perpetrated by the UMOPAR.⁵⁵ Sarcastically perhaps, the congressman also requested information about the UMOPAR's authority to collect taxes.⁵⁶

Criticism against the drug enforcers is also raised by people who disagree with the human rights advocates, with high-ranking interdiction officials complaining that these agencies lack efficacy. They claim that the Leopardos and the DEA agents do not even deal with substantial cocaine transactions that occur under their own noses, virtually across the road from the barbed-wired outposts of Chimoré, Villa Tunari, and Ivirgarzama. Enrique Valverde, local head of the State Department's Narcotics Assistance Unit (NAU) in Cochabamba until 1990, and Carlos Arauz, director of the Bolivian coca interdiction office during the Paz-Estenssoro administration, report that in February 1989, Arauz personally arrested an aircraft pilot who was making two daily flights, at 11 A.M. and 3 P.M., to collect paste. Two NAU civilian agents, a Paraguayan named Gustavo Araujo and Wilde Vega, a former prosecutor, cooperated with Arauz in intercepting the driver of the lorry carrying the money collected from paste buyers in Santa Cruz that the pilot had brought to the Chapare to buy paste. The event took place close to a village called Vueltadero only twenty minutes away from the Chimoré compound. Valverde had reported these flights to the UMOPAR and the DEA, but the DEA had refused to rely on information it had not gotten from its own informants.⁵⁷ The UMOPAR must have had different reasons for not acting because the commander of Chimoré at that time, Colonel Ricardo Molina-Viaña, looked manifestly troubled when Arauz personally handed over the spoils he had seized.⁵⁸ Several such incidents illustrate that the incompetence of Bolivian and U.S. antidrug officials did not raise concern in the high political circles of La Paz.

There was widespread chagrin in those circles when a well-known Bolivian botanist, Noel Kempff-Mercado, and two members of his research crew were assassinated in September 1986. One of the country's greatest scandals, which continued in late 1990, began when four unarmed men flew into the area to study the local flora; these three were gunned down in northern Santa Cruz by members of a cocaine hydrochloride international export network. I discuss this incident, known as the Huanchaca case, in detail in the next chapter, but it is an example of the unreliability of the enforcement agents in Bolivia. Although they had been notified of the drug traffickers' activities long before Kempff's tour, neither the UMOPAR nor the DEA tried to stop the expedition or to warn the researchers about the risk the tour involved. The DEA did not even investigate the reported laboratories despite their large size. This episode reveals that in Bolivia, the DEA follows a "stand in line and await your turn" field operations policy, thereby jeopardizing the agency's potential to cope with a large-scale drug trade. A DEA agent probably gets more credit by having in his portfolio a history of destroying four or five paste producing pits, called "factories," than one large, expensive hydrochloride processing laboratory. The reason, one may suspect, is that while overseas, the U.S. officers' interest in building a career based on "piecework" or mere "statistics"[59] overrides their commitment to their jobs. That is, much of the DEA's policy in Bolivia is dictated by its bureaucratic position within the U.S. Justice Department and the nature of career advancement within the agency rather than by the problems it was designed to address.

5. THE CROP ERADICATION EFFORT

The Bolivian administration's difficulties in implementing a cogent drug policy have been reflected in far more than simply the anomalies among enforcers. Until mid-1988, engineers from DIRECO, the technical Bolivian bureau in charge of coca eradication and substitution, utilized herbicides in spite of the government's reiterated pledge that chemicals would never be used in coca removal.[60] Peasants' allegations that the DIRECO staff had been pushed into using herbicides in the Chapare by DEA officials provoked severe unrest among the coca growers, and the turmoil escalated into open hostilities on the part of the unionized growers in the Chapare against DIRECO, the UMOPAR, and U.S. advisers in the Cochabamba district.

According to trade union leaders in the region, experiments carried out by DIRECO personnel were instigated by the *Yankis*, and in response, a belligerent campaign began with roadblocks and then an invasion of the UMOPAR outpost in Villa Tunari on June 27, 1988. According to official sources, four campesinos were killed in the clash, and two others were reported missing,[61] but eyewitnesses to the fray—trade union leaders, local journalists,[62] and politicians[63]—claim that at least twenty more unarmed peasants were drowned in the river that runs past Villa Tunari after they jumped down the slope to escape the UMOPAR and DEA's barrage. The foreign minister of Bolivia at that time, Guillermo Bedregal-Gutierrez, asserts that some peasants forcibly occupied the DEA headquarters,[64] and although this statement has not been confirmed by other sources, the Villa Tunari incident portrays the degree of violence that the presence of foreign forces can spark in the Chapare. Furthermore, it shows that Bolivian government agents had not complied with the administration's instruction to abstain from using defoliants in the eradication campaign.

The 4,000 peasants who participated in the attack[65] were organized by Julio Rocha,[66] a top union leader accused by Paz-Estenssoro officials of having close connections with the traffickers.[67] Whether the growers were driven by cocaine organizations or were spontaneously pursuing their own interests, the turmoil demonstrates that they would not surrender their coca crops without staunch resistance. The peasants were soon evicted from the UMOPAR barracks, but active hostilities ceased only when the government promised to limit its original eradication plan. The use of defoliants and herbicides in the country was expressly forbidden by an antidrug law passed on July 19, 1988, by the Bolivian Congress, which restricts legal means of coca eradication to manual procedures. As an organized force, the coca growers had shown they have enough weight to impose restraints upon government action.

The Paz-Estenssoro administration, more resolved than the previous Siles administration to fight the cocaine trade, thus found itself caught between U.S. diplomacy and a force of organized campesinos. Instead of eradicating 70 percent of the coca crop, as the United States said had been agreed, the Paz-Estenssoro administration lowered the target to 50 percent, and in reality, the expected level to be eliminated was much less. Paz-Estenssoro's foreign minister, Bedregal-Gutierrez, appealed to the Reagan administration to adopt a "more flexible" policy in order to avoid conflicts with the producers. That appeal only demonstrated that the administration of Paz-Estenssoro lacked the necessary coercive power to carry out a drastic policy to substantially reduce coca crops even if such a policy was necessary to attract U.S. aid. Nothing seems to indicate that Paz-Zamora's current administration, inaugurated in August 1989, can do any better.

6. TRANSFORMATION AMONG COCA PRODUCERS

Since the mid-1980s, relations between coca growers and cocaine businesspeople have undergone a crucial shift that makes police control of coca and coca paste even more difficult. As I have already described,[68] while enforcement efforts in the Chapare continued to stumble, the coca paste industry became in large part a cottage industry of the peasant coca growers. Today, the coca paste industry is as widespread as it is unsophisticated.

The "decentralization" of paste production, as the shift has been labeled, has two main causes, and the first relates to the effects of enforcement on small coca paste brokers. Because the demand for coca has been reduced as a result of chasing these small brokers, the price of the coca leaf is too low for the growers to make a living legally. Therefore, some peasants have been forced into cocaine manufacturing even though they were otherwise reluctant to become involved in such a risky trade.[69] The second reason for the growers' involvement in paste production stems from new policies implemented by the large traffickers. Traffickers in Santa Cruz and the Beni have realized that it benefits them to *pass on* the burdens of paste making and of transporting the paste to the large trade centers to the peasants in the Chapare, so the growers have become increasingly involved in stomping their own leaf into paste and smuggling the needed sulfuric acid and kerosene into the Chapare or purchasing the chemicals at increased costs in the local market. Thus, a large number of peasant coca growers who previously were of no concern to the Bolivian enforcement authorities are now connected with the illicit cocaine traffic. The villages of Sinahota, Ivirgarzama, Valle Sajta, Eterazama, and Isinuta are some of the depots in the Chapare, surrounding the enforcement officers' compounds, where peasants transport their cocaine sulphate.

As several reports state, the amount of land used for coca crops has grown ceaselessly. Although some victories have been claimed in the eradication campaign, it is widely admitted that 3–4 hectares are used for coca for every 1 the government manages to eliminate. An example of the expansion, the smell of coca that pervaded the air when I last visited the NAU bungalows near Villa Tunari was, as the driver explained, the result of new coca fields the agency's officials had just discovered a few weeks back.

7. SHIFTS IN U.S. POLICY

Increased enforcement has paradoxically created a decisive incentive for producing coca paste, so the size of the population that regularly transgresses the law has expanded. To avoid the economic costs and risks posed by enforcement, Camba traffickers from Santa Cruz and the Beni have transferred paste making and transport to the Kolla campesinos in the Chapare, and now that most coca growers are also small drug producers, U.S. Embassy officials in Bolivia are aware of the awkwardness of the situation. In September 1989, the U.S. ambassador to Bolivia, Robert Gelbard, told me in an interview in La Paz that a new enforcement strategy was envisaged for late 1989. According to this strategy, policing efforts would concentrate on cocaine refineries and large drug transactions. A new intelligence center would be set up in the Amazon region of the Beni to make the new strategy possible, and Robert Gelbard believed that with more accurate intelligence data, drug enforcement could be targeted at identified airfields and large laboratories instead of having the UMOPAR and the DEA flying around, squandering time and fuel, to chase coca stompers. As a part of the new policy being promoted by the U.S. Embassy, enforcement officers would overlook thousands of small producers.[70]

To implement the new policy, the ambassador also believed in the advantages of getting the Bolivian Army involved in antinarcotics operations on a regular basis, despite the standing objection that the military is as prone to become involved in the drug economy as the UMOPAR.[71] Gelbard did not discount this objection, but the embassy still espoused the view that escalating the war on drugs in Bolivia is the right step to take given the ceaseless growth of cocaine processing and trafficking. The proposed step would consist of expanding the assignment of the U.S. special forces beyond training local agents to having them join the Bolivian Army and the Leopardos in cocaine enforcement operations.[72]

By January 1990, the escalation of the war on drugs was under way, and U.S. Colonel William Depalo announced in Cochabamba in that month that Bolivian Army officers would receive training in how to combat drug trafficking at the School of the Americas in Georgia,[73] even though that military training institute has an unsavory reputation among Latin American democrats because of its role in training the worst violators of human rights in the 1970s. General Jorge Moreira-Rojas, commander in chief of the Bolivian armed forces, made it clear that this part of the plan was the result of, not just the isolated view of the ambassador, but the opinion of the State Department. According to General Moreira, the United States had conditioned its aid to Bolivia on the participation of that country's armed forces.[74]

Officers from the School of the Americas arrived in Bolivia in March 1990 to train Bolivian UMOPAR and army personnel,[75] and local officers took pride in making explicit the school's record in training officers since 1946.[76] The presence of this new set of actors contradicts a statement made by President Paz-Zamora that the Bolivian Army's intervention would be unnecessary given the existence of the special police corps,[77] the UMOPAR, but this statement, supported by Capobianco, the minister of the interior, has proved to be true. The best military officers and some police officers—Bolivian and foreign—are now selected at the Garras del Valor course in Chimoré to be sent to the School of the Americas in Georgia.[78] Nevertheless, Capobianco thought it opportune to declare to the press that the traffickers are very unlikely to overwhelm the UMOPAR's capacities and that, consequently, there is no reason to appeal to the army.[79]

Both President Paz-Zamora and Minister Guillermo Capobianco made their statements in spite of the meeting on February 14, 1990, in Cartagena of Presidents Barco, Garcia, Paz-Zamora, and Bush. According to the agreement reached at that meeting and a supplementary bilateral annex signed in May 1990, Bolivia had committed itself to engaging the army in enforcement. The events that followed the Cartagena Accord show that calling the army in was not superfluous but it was clearly negative to both internal peace in Bolivia and the international drug enforcement endeavour. I deal with this issue further in Chapter 4, where I demonstrate that adding resources to fight the war on drugs has a paradoxical effect: There is an inevitable spread of drug money contamination within a climate of paralyzing competitiveness and jealousy.[80]

8. PROBLEMS OF CONFLICTING INTERESTS: SANTA ANA

The episodes at Santa Ana de Yacuma in northeastern Bolivia in mid-1988 and 1989 strongly suggest that the U.S. Embassy's plan to engage the Bolivian Army and U.S. special forces permanently in the drug war would not only not improve enforcement in Bolivia but further complicate the scene. New actors engaging in drug enforcement, it seems, add their own conflicting interests to an already intricate situation. In mid-1988, UMOPAR agents and their DEA advisers were transported by helicopter to Santa Ana de Yacuma in the northern Beni where the notorious trafficker Jorge Roca (Techo de Paja) had been spotted. Helicopters transporting the UMOPAR agents attempted to land on a plot adjacent to the village but were forced to take off immediately when they were literally surrounded by hostile peasants who bombarded the agents with a hail of stones.[81]

Then the under-secretary of the interior, Guillermo Perez-Beltran, ordered a second attempt, and it was launched on June 23, 1989.[82] The purpose this time was to capture Hugo Rivero-Villavicencio,[83] a top drug trafficker who had mustered the hatred of his colleague Techo de Paja according to UMOPAR officers in the Chapare. This time the UMOPAR agents and their DEA advisers landed a few miles away from Santa Ana, but they could not avoid drawing fire from traffickers operating in the area as soon as they went into the village looking for Rivero-Villavicencio. The UMOPAR fired back, shooting down two of its antagonists and arresting Fernando Roca-Ali, a half brother of Techo de Paja.[84] In the middle of the shoot-out, the traffickers distributed arms among the villagers to repel the police raid. At that point, personnel from a naval base a few kilometers north of the village approached the location, and they, too, opened fire on the UMOPAR personnel, intensifying and expanding the shoot-out. A confusing battle between the Leopardos and a combination of naval forces, traffickers, and villagers ensued, and when two villagers were killed by the UMOPAR, all of the villagers engaged in the scuffle. Roca-Ali was taken away by the authorities, but Rivero-Villavicencio, rated among the six top traffickers in Bolivia by the head of the Bolivian special forces, General Añez,[85] was still at large in late 1990.[86] The toll of this UMOPAR raid was four dead and several people wounded.

Multiple factors increased the perplexity of the battle at Santa Ana de Yacuma. The outnumbered Leopardos retreated to find shelter at the naval outpost from which they had earlier been attacked, and there is also evidence that U.S. officers took an active part in the scuffle. Hugo Duque, a U.S. Air Force officer, was slightly wounded while allegedly shooting at the village from a helicopter,[87] and he received special medical attention for a scratch on his temple at Hospital Belga in Cochabamba before being evacuated to either the United States or La Paz.[88] It is unlikely that the court that probed the Santa Ana case—or anyone else—believed the excuse of the naval officer whose men had attacked the UMOPAR agents and their U.S. allies: He said he thought he was resisting a foreign invading force. However, the news that circulated in the Santa Ana region was that the Leopardos had executed a wounded peasant, leaving room for speculation about the reasons why the officer opened fire against the UMOPAR. Those reasons may have consisted of protecting the drug trade, defending the peasants' lives, or both.[89]

The version of the Bolivian enforcers is that the incident was concocted by Techo de Paja, who induced the under-secretary of the interior to dispatch the forces to Santa Ana because he sought to retaliate against Rivero-Villavicencio for having taken off some months earlier with Techo's money. The goal of the second UMOPAR/DEA assault on Santa Ana was to capture Villavicencio in such a way as to demonstrate to the other dealers in Santa Cruz that Techo had the power to manipulate enforcement and political authorities. The operation supposedly included the under-secretary who ordered it as well as UMOPAR and U.S. agents.[90] What makes this version convincing is that there were simple, inconspicuous ways to arrest Romero-Villavicencio on charges of owning a hydrochloride laboratory discovered in June 1988 on his ranch in the Beni.[91] It was common knowledge to everybody in Santa Cruz, including narcotics division officers, that Rivero-Villavicencio was a daily customer at a bar called La Pascana, and the arrest could have easily been carried out there.[92]

The second operation in Santa Ana demonstrates Techo de Paja's desire to show his clout through spectacular showdowns. As the story goes, the arrest of his half brother, Roca-Ali, was purely coincidental. Driven by curiosity, Roca had interrupted a drinking session with a friend to find out what the shooting was all about. He was immediately arrested, and his drinking companion was shot dead on the spot.

When granted a furlough by the Second Special Court of Controlled Substances in Santa Cruz, Roca did not miss the opportunity to escape.[93] A second judge declared to the press that should Roca be found guilty of drug trafficking, the prison authorities and the governor of La Paz himself would face charges for prison evasion, a specific offense foreseen in the 1988 antidrug law.[94] In September 1990, Rivero-Villavicencio was acquitted in absentia on all counts.

Santa Ana is not the only lawless town in the northern district of the Beni where villagers support cocaine traffickers. In many remote jungle areas where the weak Bolivian state has no presence, utilities such as primary education, health care, and security are provided by local caudillos whose resources derive primarily from the cocaine trade. U.S. Ambassador Gelbard is familiar with a whole list of villages near the Brazilian border that resemble Santa Ana, the village of San Ramón probably being the largest.[95]

9. BOMBINGS IN THE CHAPARE

In September 1990, while a United Nations agency was building new roads in the Chapare, the DEA staged a major campaign in the red area to disable dirt roads suspected of being used by traffickers as airstrips for pickups of coca paste. In early October, I was driven by UMOPAR agents to witness the deep craters that the DEA explosives had produced in the straight segments of the roads that link the villages of Isinuta, San Gabriel, and Eterazama, probably the most active sector of the coca paste trade in Bolivia in 1990.

In more ways than one, destroying the roads did not suit the purpose of drug enforcement, as it stepped up the existing tension between local residents and the police forces by damaging the property of those peasants who lived close to the spots that were blasted. The NAU contributed to the repair of those settlers' hovels, the facades of which had been literally blown off, but the peasants in the area were not appeased, as was proved in the last days of September. Although the DEA agents claimed that they had been attacked by traffickers, it was campesinos—male and female—who surrounded a group of eight or nine UMOPAR and DEA agents on the southern bank of the Isiboro River near Isinuta. A scuffle ensued. The fray could have ended tragically for the DEA/UMOPAR force after a shootout that lasted more than an hour, but once more, tragedy befell the peasants. A helicopter came to the rescue of the encircled officers and fired into the crowd, killing no fewer than four campesinos. Only one enforcement agent was shot in the shoulder. A burned-out UMOPAR lorry was lying in the river when I visited the place two days later.

The bombings also had extremely negative consequences for the future of enforcement in the sector. An UMOPAR captain explained to me that the damaged roads would severely hinder night raids in Isinuta and San Bernardo but would not affect the traffickers' activities. To carry on with their routine business, the cocaine dealers needed only to give the local villagers $200–$300 to build new airstrips, a task that would take only a couple of days of slashing and burning.[96] Ironically, when returning to Eterazama, we saw a bronze plaque attached to the side of a bridge a few miles away from San Gabriel. The plaque declared that the bridge and the road had been built with the effort of the people of the United States: "Peace Corps, 1968."

10. SUMMARY

In these first two chapters, I have explained how the war on drugs has backfired and actually encouraged a vast segment of the population in the Chapare to manufacture coca paste. Enforcement has actually increased drug production and blurred the image of "the enemy" by expanding the proportion of the rural population transgressing the law. Drug offenders are no longer identifiable groups from the Beni and Santa Cruz de la Sierra.

Escalation of enforcement has thus far failed. Training a special police force, the UMOPAR, has brought about contentious reactions from the army, which has succeeded in limiting the resources of the UMOPAR, thus curtailing the efficacy of that force.[97] Joint operations between the UMOPAR and U.S. personnel have also proved fruitless. Operation Blast Furnace, in which U.S. soldiers had a prominent role, was a failure not only because coordination between forces was extremely poor but also because of information leaks. In Chapter 3, I will also show through an account of the Huanchaca incident the inexplicable modus operandi adopted by the DEA and the UMOPAR.

Bolivia seems to be caught in a trap. Improving enforcement requires a stronger state, and a stronger state necessitates enforcement to rid the bureaucracy of the tangled web of interests conspiring against any move to eliminate the coca/cocaine economy. The Huanchaca case reflects the ineffectiveness of enforcement and what Anthony Henman calls the "compenetration" of cocaine traffickers and the state.[98] The same case also shows how coca/cocaine interests have so muddled the situation in Bolivia that a warlike approach is highly inefficient. According to the U.S. Embassy in Bolivia, the cocaine hydrochloride seized in 1989 may have been only 0.5–1 percent of the amount produced. If the military is deemed necessary to improve performance, the lack of cooperation among the UMOPAR, the army, and the navy should be kept in mind in trying to formulate a plausible strategy. So far, their "cooperation" has hindered interdiction.

The degree of inefficiency is underlined in a report by U.S. officials who visited Bolivia in January 1990. The report states that scuffles between the army and the UMOPAR frustrate enforcement,[99] and the observers maintain that to engage the army in drug enforcement and to expand the activities of the navy and air force would bring about the negative effect of uncontrollable internal confrontations.[100]

NOTES

1. See Steven Wisotsky, *Beyond the War on Drugs: Overcoming a Failed Public Policy* (Buffalo, N.Y.: Prometheus Books, 1990), p. 157.

2. See Chapter 4, section 4.

3. DIRECO (Direccion Regional de la Coca), founded in 1983, is a technical office under the jurisdiction of the Agrarian and Peasants Ministry. It consists of roughly 300 officials—mainly engineers, botanists, and surveyors.

4. James Van Wert, "The US State Department's Narcotics Control Policy in the Americas," *Journal of Interamerican Studies and World Affairs* 30:2–3 (Summer/Fall 1988), p. 16. (Mr. Van Wert is an official in the State Department's Bureau of International Narcotics Matters, INM.)

5. NAU top officials in La Paz think that if the UMOPAR is to remain an elite force, the number of its members must be restricted. This limitation, however, makes army intervention in enforcement crucial given that traffickers have taken over villages and entire territories (interview with the head of the NAU in Bolivia, Brian Stickney, La Paz, May 24, 1990).

6. Interview with Leopardo officer Gustavo Araujo in Chimoré, May 28, 1990. The NAU offices, distributed through the world, are under the jurisdiction of the INM, which is part of the U.S. State Department.

7. *Ultima Hora* (La Paz), August 30, 1990.

8. *Latinamerica Press*, July 26, 1984.

9. For the Diaz-Vargas entanglement with drug traffickers in 1990, see Chapter 3, section 3.

10. See *New York Times*, July 1, 1984.

11. Gigena, however, enjoys a good reputation among staunch democratic circles. According to Enrique Valverde (interview in the Chapare on September 16, 1989) and Elva Morales (interview, Cochabamba, January 15, 1990), the captain acted out of complete ignorance of what was going on.

12. Interview with Enrique Valverde on a trip to the Chapare, September 1989. Valverde, head of the NAU in the Cochabamba region until early 1990, is currently an adviser of NAU.

13. *New York Times*, July 1, 1984.

14. See Chapter 4, section 4.

15. See discussion of the feuds between the army and the police in Chapter 4, section 4.

16. I was interviewing General Añez, commander of the Bolivian special (antidrug) forces, when the general's aide announced to his boss that Major Barriga was on the phone to speak to the general (May 31, 1990).

17. See Chapter 3, section 3.

18. Meeting with Senator Hawkins at a luncheon in Washington, D.C., in early September 1988.

19. *Latinamerica Press*, July 26, 1984.

20. To my knowledge, the presidential decree was formally still in force in 1990. A lawyer devoted a great deal of time trying to find a new decree that abrogated this one, but no such decree appears to have been registered.

21. *Latinamerica Press*, December 20, 1984.

22. William Walker III claims that the expedition was funded by the United States and adds that it did not exhibit any success whatsoever (see Walker, *Drug Control in the Americas*, rev. ed. [Albuquerque: University of New Mexico Press, 1989], p. 206).

23. Arnold Trebach, *The Great Drug War* (New York: Macmillan Publishing Company, 1987), p. 170.

24. Special unpublished report of Commanders Ricardo Lopez and Jorge Vazquez, Gendarmeria Nacional Argentina, Narcotics Division Archives, 1988.

25. Kenneth E. Sharpe, "The Drug War: Going After Supply," *Journal of Interamerican Studies and World Affairs* 30:2–3 (Summer/Fall 1988), p. 77.

26. See U.S. Congress, Committee on Government Operations, "Thirty-Eighth Report: United States Anti-Narcotics Activities in the Andean Region" (Washington, D.C., August 30, 1990), p. 23, where the issue of "poor interagency coordination" is underlined.

27. Special report of Commanders Ricardo Lopez and Jorge Vazquez.

28. UMOPAR officer in the Chapare, May 25, 1990. With reference to U.S. agencies, a U.S. congressional commission has written: "The operational approaches of DEA and the Departments of State and Defense are divergent and even contradictory. . . . Absent studious coordination and oversight, these differences in approach erupt into confusion and conflict at the operational level" (U.S. Congress, Committee on Government Operations, "Thirty-Eighth Report," p. 23).

29. I officially visited their barracks in Chimoré compound in July 1988 and was later driven to an airfield some 20 kilometers from the outpost to be flown into Santa Cruz by a DEA aircraft. Personnel in combat uniforms, whom I had met in Chimoré, surrounded the airstrip, invoking security reasons. They respectfully backed off from engaging in any sort of conversation.

30. DOD rules say that the special forces cannot engage in any activity in the field that is not strictly self-defensive. Reports, however, indicate that the rules were violated in Peru when the Green Berets accompanied local personnel in their first ground operations (U.S. Congress, Committee of Government Operations, "Thirty-Eighth Report," p. 28). As far as I know, the general restraint has been respected in Bolivia.

31. On September 29, I interviewed members of the television crew in an alley in La Paz. They showed a video portraying the burning pit and also their dialogue with the DEA officer at the roadblock. Furthermore, DEA agents have bombed various roads in the Chapare, thus impeding the flow of agricultural products to the city. This deed is explained in Chapter 2, Section 8. (See Casey Vannett, "DEA Boss Authorizes Bolivians to Investigate Alleged DEA Abuses," *Times of the Americas,* June 12, 1991, p. 2.)

32. UMOPAR officers in charge of instructing the corps' personnel commented on this issue at a meeting in the outpost of Chimoré on May 29, 1990. To corroborate this view, see U.S. Congress, Committee on Government Operations, "Thirty-Eighth Report," p. 25.

33. Conversation with NAU officers Gustavo Araujo and Enrique Valverde, Chimoré, October 3, 1990.

34. In 1988, law 1008 set up the National Council for Illicit Traffic and Undue Consumption of Drugs (Consejo Nacional del Trafico Ilicito y Uso Indebido de Drogas, CONALID). The council consists of a permanent ministerial committee presided over by the minister of foreign affairs, and it rules over the executive departments responsible for crop substitution, interdiction and traffic control, and prevention of drug consumption. There are four under-secretaries in charge of executing the policies of CONALID: Social Defense (interdiction and control of narcotics traffic), part of the Ministry of the Interior; Crop Substitution (Desarrollo Alternativo) of the Agrarian Affairs Ministry; and the National Council for Prevention, part of the Public Health Ministry; and a second one from the Minister of the Interior. Each one of these departments remains administratively in its ministerial area but will follow CONALID's instructions (see *Presencia* [La Paz], September 14, 1989).

35. Interview with Robert Gelbard, U.S. ambassador to Bolivia, September 13, 1989.

36. *Ultima Hora*, December 24, 1989.

37. *Ultima Hora*, April 4, 1990.

38. See Chapter 4, section 4.

39. General Vargas asserted that the troops would not leave the Chapare rain forest, at least during the current administration. The army, for Vargas, is the guardian of Bolivia's internal security (see *Opinion* [Cochabamba], April 15, 1990). I return to this issue in Chapter 4, section 4.

40. Interviews with Enrique Valverde, May 28, 1990, and an UMOPAR officer in the Chapare, May 29, 1990.

41. Interview with an UMOPAR officer, May 29, 1990.

42. I deal with this issue further in Chapter 4, section 4.

43. *Presencia*, March 16, 1990.

44. *Presencia*, March 17, 1990.

45. An UMOPAR captain, Chimore, Chapare, May 29, 1990. However, a statement by army commander, General Jorge Moreira-Rojas, coincided with those of UMOPAR officers when he asserted that the UMOPAR is "Enduring great material difficulties" (*Ultima Hora*, January 16, 1990).

46. *Presencia*, December 12, 1990.

47. Interview with a U.S. Embassy drug official specializing in interdiction, La Paz, May 24, 1990.

48. An April 1990 INM report disclosed that new M16 assault rifles would be provided to every UMOPAR agent once the U.S.-Bolivian agreements were signed.

49. *Ultima Hora*, February 25, 1990.

50. Interview with journalist Elva Morales, Cochabamba, January 15, 1990, and conversation with two members of San Miguel's *cocaleros* union, September

16, 1989. See also William Walker III, *Drug Control in the Americas*, rev. ed. (Albuquerque: University of New Mexico Press, 1989), p. 200.

51. The Bolivian Senate probed thirty-two cases of pillage and "other abuses" in the Beni, and human rights organizations promoted the investigation of further violations. According to the Senate's spokesman, none of the charges were answered by the heads of the UMOPAR (*Presencia*, April 13, 1990).

52. *Presencia*, December 13, 1989.

53. *Presencia*, March 17, 1990.

54. See Minister Capobianco's address to UMOPAR officers in the Chapare (*Presencia*, March 16, 1990). Observers of the Chapare acknowledge today that the brunt of indiscriminate police repression is almost exclusively borne by the poor *cocaleros* and the Chapare region's labor force (e.g., Michael Painter, *Institutional Analysis of the Chapare Regional Development Project [CRDP]*, [Institute for Development Anthropology, Clark University, Worcester, Massachusetts, and Institute for Development Anthropology, Binghamton, New York, 1990], p. 42).

55. *Presencia*, October 1, 1990.

56. Ibid.

57. One of the participants in the operation made this statement to me in Chimoré on October 4, 1990.

58. Interview with a direct witness, La Paz, September 14, 1989.

59. See Michael Levine (an ex-DEA agent), *Deep Cover: The Inside Story of How DEA Infighting and Subterfuge Lost Us The Biggest Battle of the Drug War* (New York: Delacorte Press, 1990), p. 234.

60. Guillermo Bedregal-Gutierrez and Ruddy Vizcarra-Pando, *La lucha boliviana contra la narcotrafico* (La Paz: Los Amigos del Libro, 1989), p. 271. Bedregal-Gutierrez served as foreign affairs minister under President Paz-Estenssoro.

61. Videos taken by Cochabamba journalist Elva Morales show no visible sign of violence on the part of the coca growers.

62. Interview with journalist Elva Morales, Cochabamba, January 15, 1990.

63. Interviews with ex-congressman and presidential candidate Roger Cortez, La Paz, January 9 and May 21, 1990.

64. Bedregal-Gutierrez and Vizcarra-Pando, *La lucha boliviana*, p. 270. Rensselaer Lee III claims that DIRECO was invaded by a crowd of between 4,000 and 5,000 peasants looking for evidence that herbicides were being tested in the Chapare (Rensselaer Lee III, "Dimensions of the South American Cocaine Industry," *Journal of Interamerican Studies and World Affairs* 30:2–3 [Summer/Fall 1988], p. 87). It is difficult to support this thesis simply because there is no room for that number of people in DIRECO's facilities, and no other report claims that the peasants were ever inside DIRECO.

65. *Andean News*, June 3, 1988.

66. Interviews with Elva Morales, January 15, 1990, and Roger Cortez, January 9, 1990.

67. Anibal Aguilar, under-secretary for alternative development in Paz-Estenssoro's administration, formally accused Julio Rocha of being involved in drug trafficking, and as more evidence about Rocha's activities, there is Enrique Valverde's account of the helicopter inspection tour in the Chapare (see Chapter 1, section 7).

68. See Chapter 1, section 4.

69. Experts claim that campesinos are pressed by the traffickers on the one hand and by enforcement agents on the other. The "war" approach has turned the situation into a battle of interests in which the social class at the bottom, the campesinos, is the center of official and trafficker threats (see Jose Mirtembaum, a former trade union adviser, "Frente a la militarización consideramos la legalización" [unpublished paper, 1990]).

70. Interview with Ambassador Robert Gelbard at the U.S. Embassy, La Paz, September 13, 1989.

71. The same doubt disturbed a U.S. investigative committee: "What is not clear is why it will be easier to filter out corrupt elements within the military, with its legacy of involvement in drug related activities by officials of former military governments" (U.S. Congress, Committee on Government Operations, "Thirty-Eighth Report," p. 74. The candidate for the MNR and former Planning Minister Gonzalez Sanchez de Lozada stated recently: "When you have a corrupt chief of the police, you fire him. When you have a corrupt chief of the army, he fires you." Thomas Kamm, "Bolivians Fear a U.S. Led War on Drugs: American Army's Presence May Set Off Violence," *The Wall Street Journal*, June 24, 1991, p. A8. The ambassador dismissed the allegation declaring it is "a mere slogan" (ibid.).

72. At that point in time, Ambassador Gelbard went further than Assistant Secretary Ann Wrobleski on the issue of the involvement of U.S. forces in the Bolivian war on drugs. Assistant Secretary Wrobleski maintained the view that the U.S. military should confine itself to training Bolivian enforcement agents (see also Jo Ann Kawell, "The Addict Economies," *NACLA* 22:6 [March 1989], pp. 33–38).

73. *Ultima Hora*, January 19, 1990.

74. *Presencia*, March 16, 1990. Presidential adviser Samuel Doria-Medina attempted to downplay the underlying policy by stating that the military intervention would consist of building roads and other infrastructure to make alternative development possible (ibid.).

75. *Ultima Hora*, March 27, 1990.

76. What is never mentioned in Bolivia is the role of the School of the Americas in training officers of military authoritarian regimes in "interrogation techniques" and domestic intelligence. In the school, Argentineans, Guatemalans, Chileans, and officers from other dictatorial countries in the region have exchanged experiences with their U.S. colleagues. The school, based in Panama from 1977 to 1984 as a consequence of a bilateral agreement between Panama and the United States, was supposed to operate in that country for a period of ten years, but in 1985, it was provisionally moved to Fort Benning, Georgia. The school has a poor reputation among many people, and most Latin Americans view it as anathema for its part in uniting the continent's armies in many ways, one of them being efficient methods of torture (see Lars Schoultz, *National Security and United States Policy Toward Latin America* [Princeton: Princeton University Press, 1987], p. 167).

77. *Ultima Hora*, May 8, 1990.

78. Conversation among UMOPAR Captain Mario Ayala, one of the heads of the course Garras del Valor ("Clutches of Valor"); Gustavo Araujo, a Paraguayan

employee of U.S. State Department's NAU in Cochabamba; and two other UMOPAR officers at a Chimoré outpost, May 29, 1990.

79. *Ultima Hora*, May 22, 1990.

80. See Chapter 4, section 4.

81. Interview with an UMOPAR officer who participated, Villa Tunari, May 28, 1990.

82. *Ultima Hora*, March 10, 1990.

83. *Presencia*, October 1, 1990.

84. Ibid., and interview with Enrique Valverde, October 4, 1990.

85. *Ultima Hora*, March 10 and 11, 1990.

86. According to *Presencia*, October 4, 1990, Rivero-Villavicencio was acquitted in absentia earlier in 1990.

87. At the time the operation took place, U.S. helicopter pilots were training their Bolivian counterparts and allegedly became engaged in enforcement operations (Hearings, Congressional Subcommittees on Legislation and National Security and Government Information, Justice and Agriculture, October 18, 1989).

88. Interviews with a nurse from Hospital Belga; journalist Elva Morales, January 15, 1990; and a NAU employee in Cochabamba, May 23, 1990.

89. Interview with Roger Cortez, January 9, 1990.

90. Conversation with an UMOPAR captain and Gustavo Araujo, a NAU officer in Cochabamba, May 29, 1990.

91. *Ultima Hora*, March 10, 1990.

92. UMOPAR officers in the Chapare shared this common view on May 20, 1990.

93. *Presencia*, October 1, 1990.

94. Ibid.

95. Interview with U.S. Ambassador Robert Gelbard, La Paz, October 5, 1990.

96. Interview with an UMOPAR captain, San Gabriel, October 2, 1990.

97. I deal with this point in detail in Chapter 4, section 4.

98. Anthony Henman, "Cocaine Futures," in *The Big Deal: The Politics of the Illicit Drugs Business*, ed. Anthony Henman, Roger Lewis, and Tim Malyon (London and Sydney: Pluto Press, 1985), p. 155.

99. Unofficial translation of the report submitted by the Subcommittee on Information, Justice and Agriculture, presided over by John Conyers, in *Ultima Hora*, August 30, 1990. The Bolivian version tallies with the official account (U.S. Congress, Committee on Government Operations, "Thirty-Eighth Report").

100. Salient aspects of this conflict are described in Chapter 4, section 4.

3
Huanchaca

It is not conceivable that he has been shot to death; the assassins remained on the crime scene for seventy hours and when the authorities decided to act, the mobsters escaped by plane with millions of dollars in drugs, making a mockery of Justice and leaving their victims to the vultures.

The American Embassy, through the DEA and the military personnel operating jointly with that agency, had, contrary to what the U.S. Embassy has officially disclosed, knowledge and conviction of the importance of the cocaine factory.
—From the Bolivian congressional committee
in charge of investigating drug traffic
and the assassinations at Huanchaca

1. THE HUANCHACA ASSASSINATIONS

In September 1986, there was widespread chagrin in Bolivian high political circles because of the assassination of Noel Kempff-Mercado in Huanchaca[1] in the Amazonian rain forest. Flown into Huanchaca by pilot Juan Cochamanidis on an environmental and ecological research trip, Bolivian botanist Kempff-Mercado was accompanied by two other scientists, Parada and a Spaniard by the name of Vicente Castello. Huanchaca is a lush tropical plateau in the northern sector of the Department of Santa Cruz, but the research trip there should never have been allowed because clandestine large-scale cocaine traffic in the area had been formally reported to the authorities four months earlier.

In May, retired Air Force Colonel Ariel Coca-Aguirre had reported to the authorities that sizable hydrochloride laboratories and an airfield had been built in Huanchaca, and constant air traffic was perceptible, suggesting that a large drug trafficking network was operating in that place. Coca-

Aguirre had an unsavory reputation for his own suspected connections with a cocaine syndicate in Santa Cruz de la Sierra. He had once been forced to land his aircraft flying over Panama,[2] and during Garcia-Meza's cocaine dictatorship, Coca-Aguirre had played an important political role as the military regime's minister of education.[3] Coca-Aguirre's report was not taken lightly by the authorities. The DEA and the UMOPAR proceeded to corroborate the report, and on August 3, a DEA aircraft ferried Coca-Aguirre and UMOPAR officers on a reconnaissance flight over the laboratories in Huanchaca to verify the account.[4] Three large tents of the kind that is often utilized to lodge hired laborers, hundreds of drums that seemed to contain chemicals, and a shed that had all the appearance of being a hydrochloride processing laboratory were seen from the airplane.

Although the minister of the interior, the UMOPAR, and the DEA had also been informed that an armed gang was protecting the cocaine hydrochloride laboratory, no action was taken to thwart the illegal activity in Huanchaca or even to prevent the broadly announced tour of Kempff-Mercado. After landing, the group was attacked by men with automatic weapons, and Kempff-Mercado and Parada were killed outright. The pilot, Juan Cochamanidis,[5] and Vicente Castello fled to the bushes where Cochamanidis was shot to death. Castello, the only survivor of the expedition, hid in the jungle for almost sixteen hours before being rescued by a private aircraft piloted by a civilian, Mario Añez, who saw Castello waving desperately for help from an opening in the bush.

There are two puzzling aspects of the Huanchaca incident. First, the reasons why Coca-Aguirre reported the illegal activities in Huanchaca remain obscure because there are well-grounded suspicions that Coca-Aguirre himself was involved in the drug trade. Rumor even had it that his partner, a U.S. citizen known only as Lindenberg, had been arrested in the United States and charged with smuggling cocaine into that country.[6] Second, the motives behind the behavior of the DEA and the UMOPAR after the incident are also obscure. Although the authorities were notified immediately that the expedition had not returned to its base, it took the UMOPAR and the DEA over three days to arrive in Huanchaca by helicopter, and by the time they arrived, only vestiges of the dismantled refineries and an empty encampment remained. Scattered literature in Spanish, English, and Portuguese found on the spot revealed the transnational dimensions of the traffickers' network.[7]

2. THE INVESTIGATION

A Bolivian congressional committee was immediately set up to investigate the incident. When the DEA agents who had participated in the inspection were summoned to testify about what had happened, they refused to do so on the basis of their diplomatic status. Instead, the agents contributed to the investigation through the U.S. Embassy, which submitted a brief, joint presentation. The document explained that the DEA had been unable to respond immediately to the incident because "the battery in the one available helicopter needed to be replaced."[8]

Bolivian drug interests surrounding the Huanchaca affair stretched beyond the jungle of northern Santa Cruz. Active members of the congressional investigative committee received death threats to deter them from pursuing the investigation further,[9] and shortly after the committee's report had been submitted, Congressman Salazar, perhaps the foremost conductor of the probe, was assassinated in his hometown of Santa Cruz de la Sierra. It is presumed that Salazar, shot down in front of his home by two men on a passing motorcycle in the Colombian style,[10] had documents that entangled high officials of the Paz-Estenssoro administration in the Huanchaca laboratories.[11] But, unlike Colombia or Peru, violence of this kind is unusual in urban Bolivia today, and the Huanchaca case remains one of the darkest incidents in the contemporary story of the drug war in Bolivia.

3. MORE SCANDALOUS REPERCUSSIONS

Events connected to the incident continued to occur. In January 1990, officials and media investigators in Bolivia claimed that cocaine hydrochloride production in the Huanchaca area was larger than ever,[12] and that news coincided with a scandal on January 18, 1990, when Ezequiel Chavez-Justiniano, who had been arrested for his suspected primary role in the Kempff-Mercado incident, was set free from the Santa Cruz Narcotics Police headquarters by Major Diaz-Vargas. Diaz-Vargas had played a leading role in the attempted coup of 1984 when President Siles-Suazo was abducted,[13] and in 1990 he was the UMOPAR operations chief. Accused of receiving a bribe of about $50,000, Diaz-Vargas was arrested with seventeen other UMOPAR officers who were also charged with being involved in the release of Chavez.

The official version stated that on the hot Santa Cruz morning of January 16,[14] the police had raided Chavez's home in the furtherance of a court warrant issued in 1987 that ordered the arrest of Chavez for his alleged connections with the Huanchaca incident and drug manufacturing.[15] When the special prosecutor had arrived at Chavez's mansion in the Santa Cruz district of Okinawa, he had found Ezequiel Chavez-Justiniano himself, his lawyer, and Major Diaz-Vargas enjoying a steak lunch. After interrogating the detainee, the prosecutor had decided that Chavez should be held in prison. Major Diaz-Vargas had disobeyed his instructions, taking Chavez to the narcotics division of the police in Santa Cruz where he was freed.

According to Diaz-Vargas, the release was carried out on the grounds of an acquittal issued in April 1987 by Santa Cruz Judge Gilberto Roca. It was publicly known, however, that the acquittal had been appealed, thus suspending the prisoner's right to be liberated, and to quell suspicions of having been paid off, Diaz-Vargas maintained in his first version of the incident that he had been authorized to release the prisoner by his boss, Colonel Angel Cardozo, who had been appointed head of the narcotics department in Santa Cruz three days earlier.[16] Fearful that Colonel Cardozo would set the records straight, however, Diaz-Vargas corrected his version in a second statement. This time he said that Colonel Cardozo had not been consulted about the release because he, Diaz-Vargas, didn't have the colonel's home address.[17] Suspecting that his credibility was not very high and anxious to protect his "personal integrity and policeman's honor," Major Diaz-Vargas also addressed the public through a paid announcement in *Presencia*, one of Bolivia's most important newspapers. In this announcement, the police officer claimed that he had acted on the basis of the 1987 acquittal issued by Judge Roca and added that he had had no evidence that the judicial decision had been appealed.[18]

As a consequence of the Chavez scandal, the head of the Santa Cruz Narcotics Police, Colonel Cardozo, was discharged for mismanaging the force. Bismark Osinaga, the specially appointed prosecutor responsible for investigating drug offenses with the police forces, handed in his resignation in mid-January 1990, declaring that the police were unmanageable and that they constantly infringed the law. The prosecutor maintained that the contempt for the arrest warrant issued against Chavez was only one more significant example of police insubordination.[19] In late January 1990, public prosecutor Wilman Duran-Rivera pressed charges against Major Diaz-Vargas and Captains Jose Aguilera and David Murguia-Mamani for having extorted money from Chavez as a condition for setting him free.

Fifteen Bolivians charged with having participated in the Huanchaca drug trade and the assassination of Kempff-Mercado were acquitted by a trial court in Santa Cruz for lack of evidence. The acquittal also benefited Reynaldo Chavez-Justiniano, brother of Ezequiel, and two other well-known drug traffickers, Gil-Suarez and Ruiz-Añez, and a sidekick of Ruiz, Selman-Cuellar. This decision was upheld by the Santa Cruz supreme tribunal in February 1990.[20] Chief Justice Federico Fernandez-Melgar formally declared the case closed in respect to all Bolivians involved,[21] but thirteen foreigners were found guilty in absentia.[22] Because of the large probability that these foreigners did not exist, an under-secretary of justice in the Paz-Zamora administration expressed his fear that the decision eroded faith in the institutional system.[23] Given other similar experiences, it seems that creating ghosts and convicting them has become a common practice for the Bolivian judiciary. The stratagem is clearly aimed at concealing the country's lack of will to deal seriously with professional drug traffickers.[24]

The acquittal raised protests from high Bolivian officials. After the supreme court of Santa Cruz upheld the trial court's acquittal, President Paz-Zamora disclosed his misgivings on February 14, 1990, expressing concern about the lack of clarification of the Huanchaca affair and calling the judiciary's lack of effectiveness "the national weakness."[25] Congress shared the president's concern, and the chairmen of both chambers, Gonzalo Valda and Leopoldo Lopez, expressed their serious concern for what they considered a careless handling of the Huanchaca incident.[26] Although Valda stated his view that the country's Supreme Court would have to review the case,[27] Lopez claimed that the Bolivian justice system was unworthy of trust[28] and said that as a consequence, actions such as the delivery of Colonel Arce-Gomez to the DEA to be tried abroad were justified. The latter comment referred to the handing over of Garcia-Meza's principal associate, Colonel Arce-Gomez, to the DEA on December 11, 1989, to be tried in the United States.[29] According to the general opinion in Bolivia, Arce-Gomez, the minister of the interior during the one-year cocaine dictatorship, had earned the nickname of "minister of cocaine"[30] as he had organized the country's drug trade during the 1980–1981 military regime. In handing him over to the DEA, all legal procedures were sidestepped, but the case shows that the poor reputation the Bolivian justice system has earned itself abroad was fully shared by Bolivian authorities.

In an attempt to air what had happened in Huanchaca, prosecutor Wilman Duran-Rivera did not give in to the Bolivian judiciary and tried to have the acquittal invalidated, arguing that the proceedings were null and void because decisive evidence submitted to the court had been completely ignored.[31] That argument was certainly pertinent to the cases of the three well-known drug dealers—Gil-Suarez, Ruiz-Añez, and Selman-Cuellar—and Duran's assertion about the conclusiveness of the evidence gathered jointly by Bolivian and Brazilian authorities[32] seems to have been well grounded. Gil-Suarez had admitted that he had been in Huanchaca at the time of the assassination, and his personal address book had been found in a dismantled laboratory in the area. Moreover, his name was listed by traffickers as one of their paste suppliers, and according to the court's expert, the handwriting on one of the documents found at the laboratory was that of Gil-Suarez. Ruiz-Añez's name had also been found on the lists of the Huanchaca traffickers, and an associate of his had confessed that he had been hired by Ruiz to fly materials needed to produce cocaine into Huanchaca. Selman-Cuellar's responsibility was tied up to that of Ruiz in that Selman, in a Cessna 206 airplane,[33] had supplied Ruiz's laboratory with necessary materials and coca paste.[34] If the evidence was as strong as prosecutor Duran claimed, the evidence to convict the three was more than sufficient.

Prosecutor Duran was able to convince the superior tribunal of Santa Cruz to order a retrial, only to find that the Huanchaca case was too hot for the courts in Santa Cruz. After a dozen judges had excused themselves on sundry pretexts, the Huanchaca case was turned over to Judge Jaime Rivero-Aviles,[35] which raised hopes that this time justice would be inflexible. He had earned a reputation for being the toughest, most dauntless judge in Santa Cruz, feared "by rapists and murderers."[36] Thus, it came as a shock when on March 22, seven days after receiving the files, Judge Rivero-Aviles granted habeas corpus writs submitted by both Ezequiel and Reynaldo Chavez-Justiniano.[37] The warrant set Reynaldo Chavez free and mandated that the police cease to chase his brother Ezequiel, who had already been liberated by Major Diaz-Vargas under the questionable circumstances discussed above.[38] On the verge of his release, Reynaldo Chavez-Justiniano did not scrimp in offering his acquaintances a jubilant celebration. Hosting every prison inmate and warden, Reynaldo had some of his cattle slaughtered for a huge barbecue and beer party at the Santa Cruz jail.

Local prosecutor Yalila Facusses appealed the decision, declaring that the habeas corpus writs flagrantly contradicted the Bolivian law in force,[39] and Under-Secretary of Justice Roger Pando reacted strongly against the judge's decision. He claimed that in releasing Reynaldo Chavez-Justiniano, the judge had made state prosecutors lose the battle against cocaine traffic.[40] In response to a Supreme Court indictment for irregular behavior, Judge Rivero-Aviles stated that his colleagues were a bunch of cowards who had not dared decide the matter of the Chavez brothers' writs of habeas corpus,[41] and he claimed that by having him answer to charges of irregularities, the Supreme Court would bar him from trying the case.[42]

In an attempt to make up for what was viewed as a judicial scandal, the executive branch proposed the creation of new courts in order to replace judges of controlled substances; it also ordered that private airplanes in Santa Cruz and the Beni be subjected to chemical tests to establish if the aircraft had been transporting cocaine. Congress also reacted by announcing that private fortunes would be investigated. Under-Secretary Pando announced the creation of "supercourts," which would specialize in handling the cases of organized drug traffickers. The present justice system, Pando explained, was being tough only on coca growers and stompers and small coca paste manufacturers.[43] Important traffickers, he added, were treated with extreme leniency.[44]

The government's testing for traces of cocaine in small planes demonstrated that Pando's skepticism was well founded: Six small airplanes were seized, and four pilots were arrested on charges of cocaine trafficking.

However, the proceedings were once again successfully challenged. The private pilots' union (Asociacion de Pilotos Civiles) took a strong stance against the government and threatened that the pilots would go on strike indefinitely if the measures against the pilots and the seizures were maintained. The union also declared that the minister of aeronautics was responsible for their colleagues' fate and consequently declared him persona non grata. The administration decided to review the decision given the prominence of the members of the union who were also ranchers and industrialists from the Beni and Santa Cruz de la Sierra.[45]

Responding to the pilots' declared animosity, the minister of aeronautics decided to step aside in order to reach a settlement with the pilots' union. He therefore commissioned Colonel Antelo, director of civilian aeronautics, to negotiate a peace with the pilots on behalf of the ministry. Julio Antelo immediately went to Santa Cruz where he promised to have the arrested pilots released and have an amendment to the antidrug law passed in order to make it possible to return the sequestered aircraft.[46] His promises were kept.

The idea of probing the origin of conspicuous fortunes also resulted in setback for the antidrugs cause. One of the first targets of the investigation was General Hugo Banzer-Suarez, who had been Bolivia's dictator from 1971 to 1978. As the head of the Acción Democrática Nacionalista (ADN, Nationalist Democratic Alliance), the country's third political force, Banzer was one of the most important politicians in Bolivia. Even so, he came under attack from a Santa Cruz brewer Max Fernandez, who was being groomed by the ruling party, (Movimiento de Izquierda Revolucionaria, MIR), to succeed President Paz-Zamora.[47] Fernandez maintained that if dubious Bolivian fortunes were to be investigated, Banzer's wealth would have to be the first one probed. The general's assets, Fernandez claimed, originated in cocaine trafficking. Fernandez did not add anything new to an old popular suspicion,[48] but combined with previous misgivings, the new accusations made Banzer's political defenders sound purely rhetorical when they solemnly declared that the general's reputation should be cleansed "for the sake of the general, his party, and the nation."[49] Banzer's ADN party committee said the accusations were "groundless and cowardly."[50]

As is not uncommon in Bolivia, events turned against the accuser, Max Fernandez, who was himself indicted of having built his own fortune from the illicit drug business. The Brazilian news network O Globo disseminated the word that Fernandez's financial status and political reputation would soon be thwarted by allegations from the United States that his "empire had been built through connections with drug traffickers."[51] The attempt to probe into illicit fortunes was thus neutralized by later developments that wound up confusing the drug issue with partisan politics. The first vice-president of the Chamber of Deputies, Leopoldo Lopez, publicly acknowleged the legislature's inability to get such investigations off the ground.[52]

4. IN CONCLUSION

The Huanchaca case and its aftermath show that nothing seems to have changed with regard to controlling the country's drug traffic. Bolivia's Supreme Court turned down the final appeals, and when impeachment proceedings against the five Santa Cruz judges who had tried the case were defeated, all possible hopes were brought to an end.[53] Relatives and friends of the victims are still striving to clarify the incident in order to seek redress at the Interamerican Court of Human Rights.

Official U.S. opinion about the progress made in Bolivia—necessary if the country is to qualify for further aid—is that at best, it is unrealistic.[54] New laws and the appointment of more efficient and uncontaminated local officials are no sign of improvement but a mere facade. What President Paz-Zamora called Bolivia's "weakness," its justice system, is only the visible tip of an unmanageable world, and in Chapter 5, I address the relationship between Bolivia's institutional weakness and the conception of corruption in order to assess the limits of the war on drugs.[55]

It seems too optimistic, amid the series of failures to impose legal rules in force, to label Roberto Suarez-Gomez's detention in July 1988 as "the apprehension of the king," as a former minister of foreign affairs does in his book.[56] Bolivian police personnel and U.S. agents[57] have different theories about Suarez's being ostracized from the cocaine networks. His addiction to drugs and his alleged enmity with the leading coca trader of the new generation, namely, Techo de Paja, are the two dominant theories to explain his isolation.

Frustration has driven the United States and Bolivia into escalating the war on drugs. One step in this direction is the direct involvement of the Bolivian Army in drug enforcement—as was agreed by President Bush and his Andean country colleagues at the meeting held in February 1990 in Cartagena—but as I discuss in Chapter 4, this new element only brings about extra sources of conflict and generalized frustration in both administrations. In the next chapter, I also provide further examples of conflicting sectorial interests that neutralize enforcement efforts, and I tackle the special way in which the different interests involved in the coca/cocaine economy, including U.S. interests, generate insurmountable dilemmas. An explanation of the situation in Bolivia in late 1990 is provided in Chapter 5, where I explore the sources and nature of these dilemmas and the way they relate to the war approach.

NOTES

1. Also called Caparuch.

2. Interview with Kempff-Mercado's pilot's son, Hugo Cochamanidis, appointed head of the Dirección Nacional de la Coca by the Paz-Zamora administration, La Paz, September 28, 1990.

3. See James Dunkerley, *Rebellion in the Veins: Political Struggle in Bolivia 1952–1982* (London: Verso, 1984), p. 328. In fact, it is suspected that the reason Coca-Aguirre had to report the laboratories was one of "piracy," which, in the jargon of the traffickers, means being displaced from one source of supply of coca leaf or paste by new dealers (interview with Julio Alem, a sociologist researcher from Cochabamba, May 27, 1990).

4. Colonel Coca-Aguirre testified to this fact before the Bolivian congressional investigative committee on September 13. In his September 15 deposition, Colonel Honorio Ramirez supported Coca-Aguirre's version of the facts (Ramirez was the Director Departamental del Control de Substancias Peligrosas del Departamento de Santa Cruz de La Sierra). The data were also corroborated by ex-congressman and presidential candidate Roger Cortez, who had a prominent role on the committee, in an interview in La Paz, January 11, 1990.

5. Juan Cochamanidis was the father of Hugo Cochamanidis, Paz-Zamora administration's head of the Dirección de la Coca.

6. See the drafted resolution, signed by ten legislators, of the Bolivian congressional investigative committee of October 1986.

7. Material is from a report of the Bolivian congressional investigative committee.

8. Interview with a NAU agent in Cochabamba, January 14, 1990. This version was corroborated by a member of the investigative committee, Roger Cortez, in La Paz, on January 11, 1990.

9. Interview with Roger Cortez, January 9, 1990.

10. Guillermo Bedregal-Gutierrez and Ruddy Vizcarra-Pando, *La lucha boliviana contra la agresion del narcotrafico* (La Paz: Los Amigos del Libro, 1989), p. 154. See also Kevin Healy, "Coca, the State, and Peasantry in Bolivia, 1982–1988," *Journal of Interamerican Studies and World Affairs* 30:2–3 (Summer/Fall 1988), pp. 105–126.

11. Interview with Hugo Cochamanidis, September 28, 1990.

12. Interviews with Cochabamba journalist Elva Morales, January 15, 1990, and Enrique Valverde, former head of NAU in Cochabamba and currently adviser to the agency, January 17, 1990.

13. See Chapter 2, section 1.

14. *Presencia* (La Paz), January 21, 1990.

15. *Presencia*, January 23, 1990.

16. *Presencia*, January 18, 1990.

17. *Presencia*, January 23, 1990.

18. Ibid.

19. *Ultima Hora* (La Paz), and *Presencia*, January 19, 1990.

20. *Ultima Hora*, February 15, 1990.

21. *Ultima Hora*, February 10, 1990.

22. *Ultima Hora*, February 8, 1990.

23. Ibid.

24. This opinion was given to me by lawyer Armando Aquino-Huerta on May 24, 1990. Aquino-Huerta was a prosecutor for controlled substances until 1986 and is currently an adviser to the DEA in La Paz. The same opinion was given to me by a former judge of controlled substances, Miguel Arteaga-Aranibar, La Paz, September 14, 1989, and ex–special drug law prosecutor Wilde Vega, currently working for NAU, Villa Tunari, September 16, 1989.

25. *Ultima Hora*, February 15, 1990.

26. *Ultima Hora*, February 10, 1990.

27. Ibid.

28. Ibid.

29. Arce-Gomez was arrested on December 11, 1989, at his home in the lowland city of Santa Cruz and flown to the United States by DEA officials without formalities (*Presencia*, December 12, 1989).

30. See Steven Wisotsky, *Beyond the War on Drugs: Overcoming a Failed Public Policy* (Buffalo, N.Y.: Prometheus Books, 1990), p. 156.

31. *Ultima Hora*, February 4, 1990.

32. Under the headline "Hope Reborn in Huanchaca," prosecutor Duran claimed that enough evidence existed to convict Gil-Suarez, Ruiz-Añez, and Selman-Cuellar (*Ultima Hora*, February 19 and 20, 1990).

33. *Ultima Hora*, February 19, 1990.

34. *Ultima Hora,* February 4, 1990.
35. *Ultima Hora,* March 16, 1990.
36. *Ultima Hora,* March 22, 1990.
37. Ibid.
38. *Ultima Hora,* March 23, 1990.
39. Ibid.
40. *Ultima Hora,* April 4, 1990.
41. *Ultima Hora,* March 25, 1990.
42. Ibid.

43. An ex–controlled substances judge, Miguel Arteaga-Aranibar, complained to me that during his tenure in office, all he had to deal with was coca stompers and small carriers and that the police delivered only petty, poor transgressors. "Sentenced offenders belong to the lowest strata of the Bolivian society. Prisoners crowding Bolivian jails are peasants producing basic paste or petty traffickers. They are all underdogs" (interview at the Argentinean Embassy in La Paz, September 14, 1989).

44. *Presencia,* April 4, 1990.
45. Interview with Hugo Cochamanidis, La Paz, September 18, 1990.
46. *Presencia,* May 8, 1990.
47. According to the *Economist,* economic stagnation in Bolivia was increasing Max Fernandez's populist appeal and his chances of defeating the more conservative Gonzalo Sanchez de Lozada (*Economist,* October 20, 1990).

48. If the general had not been in the cocaine business personally, it is evident that he at least acquiesced to having his relatives and friends devote themselves to dealing in drugs (see Chapter 4, section 4). Furthermore, the origin of the Bolivian cocaine trade may be traced to loans granted by official banks, and observers claim that there is no way General Banzer could have ignored the development of the Santa Cruz–Beni-Chapare cocaine network (Dunkerley, *Rebellion in the Veins,* p. 318).

49. Words of Bolivian Congressman Guido Camacho in *Ultima Hora,* February 17, 1990.
50. *Ultima Hora,* February 16, 1990.
51. Reuters, Brasilia, April 11 (published in *Ultima Hora,* April 12, 1990).
52. *Ultima Hora,* February 18, 1990.
53. Hugo Cochamanidis, son of the pilot killed in Huanchaca, said to me that, legally, the case has been sealed (interview in La Paz, September 28, 1990).
54. See *International Narcotics Control: The President's March 1, 1989, Certification for Foreign Assistance Eligibility and Options for Congressional Action* (Washington, D.C.: U.S. Government Printing Office, 1989).
55. Chapter 5, section 3.
56. Bedregal-Gutierrez and Vizcarra-Pando, *La lucha boliviana,* p. 162.
57. Interviews with NAU official Enrique Valverde, Villa Tunari, May 30, 1990, and UMOPAR Captain Mario Ayala, Chimoré, May 29, 1990.

4

Bureaucracies at Their Worst

Due to the risks of corruption inherent in repressive actions against narco-traffic, the army will only participate in such actions in case of extreme necessity, but will support in any event activities designed by the government related to prevention and alternative development, said the Commander in Chief of the Armed Forces, General Jorge Moreira-Rojas.
—La Paz newspaper *Ultima Hora*, January 16, 1990

The Commander in Chief of the Bolivian Armed Forces, Jorge Moreira, reported that the United States have conditioned military aid to the direct involvement of said military institution in the struggle against narco-traffic.
—La Paz newspaper, *Presencia*, March 16, 1990

1. THE APPEAL OF PARADOXES

If the description of the social, cultural, and economic state of the Chapare today has been persuasive and the narrative about drug enforcement convincing, there is an unavoidable air of paradox throughout both. By paradox I mean a contradiction that results from a correct deduction stemming from two congruous premises. Paradoxes have a historical appeal, being often presented as games of mental skill, a challenge to logicians, or a quandary to both psychiatrists and anthropologists as an unending source of hidden conflict for the actors caught in them.[1] It is in the last sense that I find dealing with paradoxes an inevitable step in the approach to understanding the meaning of political discourse and action in the Bolivian war on drugs. A list of these perplexing paradoxes can be derived from the first three chapters of this book:[2]

1. Chapter 1 shows that the drug enforcement campaign in Bolivia is characterized by the fact that active policing of drug production and trade

causes a substantial increase in the manufacturing and marketing of cocaine. Specifically, trading in basic paste by the settlers in the Chapare region has consistently continued to increase since the war started.

2. In Chapter 2, I argue that the more crucial the UMOPAR police corps became to waging the war, the less efficient the force became because of a lack of communications equipment, adequate weaponry, and means for a decent livelihood—some of these men lack mattresses, adequate nourishment, sanitary facilities, and so on. Furthermore, as more agencies add their "contribution" to drug enforcement, the more inefficient this "common" effort becomes, and the more entangled the situation winds up being. Good examples of this paradox are the cases of Santa Ana de Yacuma and Operation Blast Furnace.

3. The Huanchaca case described in Chapter 3 demonstrates the inappropriateness of the commonsense principle that more importance must be attached to the most important issues. This axiom is not applicable to the strategy to control drugs in Bolivia.

These singled-out contradictions are not a coincidence but the necessary response to structural features of enforcement. In Chapter 5, I attempt to explain the factors that lead to paradoxical behavior; in this chapter, I supply three more examples of what seems to be simple nonsense and demonstrate that dealing with such events is essential to understanding the antidrug environment. The first of these cases took place in 1989 and suggests that U.S. bureaucrats operate by different criteria in varied contexts. Learning from the Bolivian experience will dispel the belief that a strong, efficient, and "ethical" U.S. state apparatus is confronted with the difficulties of dealing with corrupt officials from weak, inefficient states abroad. The other two sets of events took place in 1990, and illustrate the point that intensifying efforts, either by taking enforcement more seriously or by increasing the number of participants, leads to undesired consequences.

These three cases concern, first, the episode of the 156 missing hectares and the 1989 coca eradication program in Bolivia (section 2, "Who Is Cheating on Whom?"); second, bringing down the price of coca and the undesired drop of seizures and arrests (section 3, "If You Want to Succeed, Avoid Success"); and third, the dubious reasons for engaging the army in drug enforcement and the still more dubious prospect that the Bolivian Army will ameliorate the country's antidrug campaign (section 4, "Who Wants to Bring the Good Old Army In?"). The political role Latin American armies have played in their own countries' politics and the peculiarities of Bolivia's history suggested that the last section should be split into three parts: "The Logic of Militarizing Enforcement," "The Political Dilemma," and "The New War: The Army Versus the Police."

2. WHO IS CHEATING ON WHOM?

Since 1982, the U.S. and Bolivian governments have agreed upon the amount of coca to be eradicated by the latter with the aid of the former.[3] In 1987, the PIDYS[4] plan replaced the 1985 triennial plan for eradication and substitution,[5] and according to this new plan, Bolivia committed itself to eliminating 5,000 hectares of coca yearly. The reasons why DIRECO, the Bolivian office specializing in eradication,[6] has never met the envisaged annual quota are a source of discrepancy between Bolivians and Americans, who have different opinions about the allotment of responsibility for the failure. Bolivian officials, and DIRECO's personnel in particular, blame the U.S. Embassy for its failure to supply punctually the necessary resources to carry out the assignment. The major claim Bolivian officials have against the U.S. Embassy's staff is that it manipulates the funds that are allocated to eradication campaigns. Every year, Bolivians say, NAU's administrative officials do whatever it takes to hold the funds allotted to coca eradication until September 30, the end of the fiscal year for the U.S. bureaucracy. Thus, the embassy comptrollers get credit for saving U.S. Treasury's money. In January 1990, one UMOPAR officer asserted that the embassy's strategy consisted of delaying every cash delivery until September because "saving fiscal money is likely to result in promotions. U.S. officers do not give a damn about Bolivia; they will soon leave the country anyway, and once they are gone the only thing that counts for them is their own status in the DEA or NAU."[7]

Not surprisingly, officials in the U.S. Embassy have a different view: Bolivia has never accomplished its commitments, and nothing indicates that things will change. Corruption and a generalized inefficiency make cooperation with the Bolivians almost impossible.[8] Supported by some Bolivians, Americans claim that local officials are unable to come up with reasonable projects to justify NAU's financial support.

In either event, officials of both countries recognize that to date, there has been a lack of basic information needed by Americans and Bolivians in order to carry out an effective plan of coca removal. No plan is feasible as long as nobody can say how many man hours it takes to eradicate a planted hectare, and so far, there have been no data concerning this topic.[9]

To improve the poor record in coca elimination, a proposal to split the yearly program into a two-stage commitment was submitted by NAU officials to the Bolivian authorities. The plan consisted of dividing the year 1989 into two periods and establishing an elimination quota for each phase. Between January 1 and July 23, the Bolivian government would be expected to eradicate 1,300 hectares. In July, once that commitment had been met, the U.S. Embassy would contribute $5,400,000 for further eradication. As it turned out, Bolivia could not honor even this short-term agreement.

On July 22, an emissary of Anibal Aguilar-Gomez, under-secretary of alternative development, met with DIRECO officers in the Chapare at their office near the village of Villa Tunari. At this meeting, it was revealed that the eradication campaign had fallen 156 hectares short of the expected 1,300 hectares. On the assumption that the shortcoming would hamper further aid from the United States, Aguilar's spokesman came up with the idea that the maps be modified and additional reports written to cover the missing 156 hectares.[10] After emphasizing the importance of obtaining the $5.4 million in assistance from the United States, the under-secretary's representative stressed the necessity of presenting documentation to show that the whole 1,300-hectare plan had been carried out. To convince the head of DIRECO, Zamendo, the under-secretary's emissary, made a successful appeal to patriotism.

As word about the ploy reached NAU officials in Cochabamba, Zamendo was warned not to go ahead with the maneuver or else a report of the fabrication would be filed in the central NAU office at the U.S. Embassy in La Paz, but the warning did not deter DIRECO personnel from altering the maps. NAU officials in Cochabamba sent a formal report to La Paz, but surprising to the NAU officials in Cochabamba, officials at the U.S. Embassy did not acknowledge the information against Zamendo and Aguilar and proceeded to approve DIRECO's account, filing the corresponding report in Washington.[11]

As a consequence of the documents submitted by Zamendo's team and the ensuing report from the U.S. Embassy to Washington, the Bolivian government's eradication obligation for the January–July period was considered fulfilled, and the ploy went almost unnoticed. Aguilar and Zamendo were personally given credit for their good job in the eradication campaign, and in all likelihood, the reputation of the top NAU officials in La Paz also improved. One may conclude that officials of the INM[12] in Washington must have judged that the officials in charge in Bolivia had demonstrated how the embassy there could make use of its clout to further U.S. interests in Bolivia. As it happened, the alteration of the facts ended up personally benefiting all the people involved in the war on drugs in Bolivia.

The maneuver was not invisible to everybody. After the Paz-Zamora administration succeeded Paz-Estenssoro's in August 1989, Bolivian Congressman Guido Camacho addressed the press on January 20, 1990, to condemn the 156-hectare case. Clearly referring to that episode, Camacho stated that the country lacked sufficient means to annually rid itself of 5,000 hectares of coca. He also indicted the Paz-Estenssoro administration for having determined the amount of removed coca "under pressure and with irresponsible optimism."[13]

In the aftermath of the 156-hectare episode, Zamendo was rewarded for his performance. In 1990, he became an adviser to the U.S. Embassy in La Paz and was commissioned to control the eradication campaign,[14] under Brian Stickney, the head of NAU in Bolivia. In May 1990, Javier Alvarez was appointed to the top position in DIRECO. A man with an opprobrious reputation for his connection with the paramilitary groups of Garcia-Meza's cocaine dictatorship,[15] it is also known that Alvarez had increased his personal wealth substantially during the military regime.[16] Conversely, in early 1990, NAU officers who had attempted to prevent the stratagem were demoted, and, as a possibly connected event, Enrique Valverde was removed from his post as the head of the NAU in Cochabamba and given a secondary role as an adviser in the region, and more specifically in the Chapare. Valverde's successor in the Cochabamba office of NAU was an American ex–police officer by the name of Cepeda. He has earned himself a poor reputation—UMOPAR officers whom I met in the Chapare claimed that Cepeda had hardly inspected the critical province at all.[17]

The case of the 156 missing hectares shows that within the war on drugs scheme, policing officials find that they fare better if they turn their heads than if they actually control the targeted problem. The conclusion that the story suggests is that rewards are not granted to the people who endeavor to pursue their duties but to those who help present a positive image to the U.S. Congress and public so that U.S. funds will continue to flow—that is, those who are willing to go along with an acknowledged fiction. In the war on drugs, harmony between U.S. and Bolivian bureaucrats often depends on the ability to overlook irregularities. The case of the missing 156 hectares shows not only that cheating can benefit the chiseler and his group but also that on a certain level, U.S. and Bolivian officials are likely to share goals that are often incompatible with those of the countries they represent. The next two sets of events confirm this view.

3. IF YOU WANT TO SUCCEED, AVOID SUCCESS

The under-secretary of the interior in the Paz-Zamora administration, Raul Loaysa-Montoya,[18] and the deputy under-secretary of social defense, Jorge Torrico,[19] are only two of a number of high Bolivian officials who believed that 1990 was a successful year in the Bolivian drug enforcement and eradication campaigns. February and May of 1990—they claimed— were two months that showed how low the price of coca may fall as a result of relentless enforcement. According to NAU officials in La Paz,

3,461 hectares had been eradicated in the Chapare by late April, more than duplicating the previous year's performance.[20] In May, Bolivian officials assert, settlers were abandoning the Chapare region to return to their homelands as the value of coca had dropped precipitously from over 100 bolivianos a load (or *carga*)[21] to less than 20.

The optimism of many Bolivian officials was shared by the majority at the U.S. Embassy. U.S. policymakers concerned with the coca/cocaine suppression campaign claimed that a number of peasants were dropping out of that trade in the Chapare. "It is difficult to find [coca harvest] pickers these days. Some [peasants] would even walk away from their green crops" declared one top-ranked U.S. specialist.[22] A drop of 80 percent in the usual level of beer consumption in the Chapare was seen as an unequivocal sign of progress in quelling coca growing and paste manufacturing. The sizable number of street vendors' permits requested in the region's capital city of Cochabamba was another sign of the policy's success in 1990.[23]

Not every Bolivian and U.S. Embassy official shared this optimistic view, however. A few were still skeptical about the accomplishments of the enforcement and eradication efforts, and some did not believe the veracity of the disclosed figures of arrests, seizures, and number of eradicated hectares.[24] The disbelief of some people could be attributed to their tacit or expressed rejection of the overall approach of the war on drugs more than to the 1990 campaign alone.[25] Furthermore, not all of the parties involved in the campaign were able to relish the celebrated outcome because the slump in the price of coca affected the volume of coca/cocaine sales in the Chapare in both February and May. Some *cocaleros* refused to sell their harvests or to turn them into paste, which had two consequences. The first, direct consequence was a halt in coca/paste transactions; the second, indirect effect was a drop in the number of arrests and seizures made by the UMOPAR. This latter development was bad news for some U.S. officials involved with the war on drugs in Bolivia.

A few days after the price reached its low point in May, the situation in the Chapare changed radically. On May 28, 1990, I met with two peasants in Villanueva,[26] a hamlet near the Chapare's red area where cocaine paste is intensely produced. After refusing to provide any information that might indicate they were involved in the cocaine trade, both Chapareños revealed that in the past few days, the price of a load of coca had soared from 15 to 120 bolivianos. One of them added that in Eterazama,[27] a village that is some 20 kilometers east of Villanueva, a load was quoted at 140 or even 160 bolivianos. This news was later verified by UMOPAR and NAU officers. Such swings are the result of a host of variables, most of which are linked to the consuming market, but developments in February 1990 added a new, local reason for the abruptness of the May oscillation. The reason stems from the existing ties between the UMOPAR and the NAU's leading officials in La Paz.

In February 1990, after the coca leaf had reached its lowest price, the NAU summoned UMOPAR officers to the U.S. Embassy in La Paz. At a meeting with DEA and USAID officers, the head of NAU, Brian Stickney, expressed his dissatisfaction at the poor performance of the UMOPAR. Arrests and seizures of coca/cocaine were too poor, regardless of the depression that the drug trade in the Chapare was undergoing, and the embassy was ready to levy penalties on the Leopardos should they not improve their performance. In 1989, the NAU office in La Paz had decided to withhold the $50 monthly bonus given to UMOPAR agents to deter them from performing too few arrests and seizures, and with the acquiescence of the DEA, NAU's top official in the country now threatened to penalize the UMOPAR once again if the current trend continued.[28] Given that the $50 bonus was equivalent to a Leopardo's monthly official earnings, the threat had a serious impact on the UMOPAR officers at the meeting. It is reasonable to infer either that a similar warning was circulated in May or simply that the February threat was sufficiently deterring to make a second one unnecessary. It is clear that arrests and confiscations to report to Washington were essential to the NAU in La Paz, but it is difficult to see why since the United States has expressed time after time that its strategy in the Andean countries is centered in lowering the price of coca in order to drive growers away from the trade.[29]

If policing coca/cocaine activities is aimed largely at lowering the value of coca, the February and May events reflect a genuine dilemma and lead to the conclusion that being successful at law enforcement is incompatible with making law enforcement unnecessary (by helping bring cocaine operations to a halt). It is true that a drop in coca/cocaine prices is also likely to derive from circumstances other than enforcement itself. Top NAU officials in La Paz, for instance, attribute the May slump to the invasion of Panama by the United States in December 1989, the assassination of presidential candidate Luis Carlos Galán in Colombia in the same year, and economic cycles that the cocaine trade invariably experiences.[30]

By the end of September 1990, the price of a load of coca had reached 260 bolivianos. A skirmish between traffickers and peasants against the UMOPAR and DEA in Isinuta on September 29 and what were considered successful police raids in Santa Cruz brought the price down to 70 bolivianos by October 2, but on October 4, the price had again risen to 120 or 140 bolivianos depending on the venue.

4. WHO WANTS TO BRING THE GOOD OLD ARMY IN?

THE LOGIC OF MILITARIZING ENFORCEMENT

Coca growing and cocaine trafficking relentlessly increased in Bolivia during the 1980s in spite of enforcement efforts to thwart them. Many people believe, and U.S. policy maintains, that the war on drugs is being lost for lack of resources. This view holds that bringing the Bolivian Army into the war is appropriate, and although the U.S. government maintains this position, Latin Americans have persistently demurred. At the Cartagena meeting in February 1990, the Bolivian administration did agree to engage its army in drug enforcement, yet this move does not reflect the Bolivian political view of the matter. Bolivian and other Latin American critics of militarizing the war on drugs have substantial arguments to support their disagreement with the U.S. policy, and a look at the progress made in Bolivia as a result of that policy provides evidence that these critics are right, but for more reasons than those they have expressed.

At a November 13, 1987, meeting of the American armies held in the Argentinean city of Mar del Plata, the Latin American representatives reached a consensus about the overriding drawbacks of engaging a country's armed forces in drug enforcement. The Bolivian delegates agreed: Despite the assertion (unsubstantiated) that drug trafficking is strongly connected to radical terrorists,[31] the military should not be directly involved in drug enforcement. Only the Chileans, representing the last military regime in the Southern Cone,[32] supported the U.S. proposal that the region's armies should be deployed to combat drug trafficking.

Several reasons were given as to why the military should be kept out of the war on drugs, one being that corruption is likely to undermine the soldiers' morale and disrupt discipline. In the 1970s, U.S. national security doctrine had driven Latin American armies to wage "dirty wars" against radical insurgency, and the resulting confusion of police and army roles had proved costly. Antisubversion campaigns had resulted in massive violations of human rights, politicization of military officers' cadres, and the extreme unpopularity of the armies in the Southern Cone.

Indeed, at the meeting in Mar del Plata, a large majority of the Latin American military people believed in the "staircase theory," which claims that all evils requiring repression should be dealt with at the lowest possible level of government.[33] Considering that the military is their countries' last—and loftiest—resource, there would be no purpose in engaging military personnel in any struggle that the police forces should be able to handle. For most high-ranking military officers, the most attractive policy consisted of discreetly removing the armed forces from most of the conflicts related to noninsurgent criminal activities.[34]

When the U.S. war on drugs advocates persisted, the weak and transitional Latin American civilian administrations demanded a serious assessment of the danger that such a war might provoke institutional collapse. They worried that involving armies in the policing of drug traffickers would inescapably have undesirable consequences, and they saw two possible outcomes. One, and most improbable, an army might succeed in thwarting drug trafficking and consumption, but such success would give the generals little incentive to let the politicians govern, as it could then be argued that they were incapable of achieving what only the armed forces could accomplish. As drugs had been formally labeled an issue of national security since the mid-1980s,[35] the ability of civilian governments to manage the countries' most delicate internal affairs would then be disputed. Some Latin American administrations, such as that of Mexico, made this point explicit.[36] Two, if a country's armed forces failed to quell illicit drug activities, their inability to confront issues of national security would be exposed to potential enemies.[37] These arguments are familiar to U.S. politicians who adhere to the 1878 Posse Comitatus Act, which prohibits the military from engaging in internal enforcement and presumes that democracy is safeguarded by the distinction between enforcement and defense.[38]

Other grounds for resisting military intervention stem from three dangerous dynamics of Latin American military history: one, the lingering proneness of a number of highly ranked officers to get along with cocaine businesspeople; two, a demonstrated readiness to abuse the rights of peasants; and three, the long-standing nationalism that makes direct cooperation with the United States impracticable (indeed, the 1982 Falklands/Malvinas experience has made Latin American militaries especially cautious about the sturdiness of alliances established with their North American comrades). Furthermore, the commanders of the Bolivian armed forces had additional reasons for not engaging in drug enforcement in their country. Pictures of soldiers stomping coca leaves and of army lorries carrying heaps of basic paste during General Garcia-Meza's cocaine dictatorship still circulate among politicians, trade union leaders, and students and hamper the army's legitimacy in the contemporary move to establish democracy.[39] Cocaine trafficking emerged in Bolivia, not solely as the result of opportunistic entrepreneurs in the private sector, but under the aegis of military dictatorships, and this fact affects the military's current reputation and its role in a civilian-run state.

Although Bolivia has had over 200 military coups, the combination of government violence and the drug entanglement of top political officials may be traced to General Hugo Banzer's dictatorship from 1971 to 1978, the period in which the cocaine business in Bolivia took off. In 1990, General Banzer came under attack when Max Fernandez insinuated that

Banzer's wealth stemmed from the cocaine business.[40] Although Banzer's supporters defended him,[41] it seems clear that if the general was not personally involved in the cocaine business, he had at least looked the other way when his relatives and friends exported cocaine.

The Banco de Crédito Agrícola of Santa Cruz played a key role in the setting up of the Santa Cruz–Chapare coca/cocaine enterprise after the cotton industry in Bolivia collapsed in the mid-1970s,[42] and observers claim that there is no way that the government, including General Banzer himself, could have ignored the commencement of this cocaine business. The general had strong ties with Santa Cruz financial sectors,[43] and it is also maintained that Banzer threw thousands of peasants in the area off their land to make more room for agribusiness while deploying the military to quash strikes in the mines.[44] To make the general's situation even more suspicious, his son-in-law Luis Valle was expelled from Canada after being found in possession of cocaine,[45] and his nephew and private secretary were arrested in Miami and Canada on drug charges.[46]

The Banzer regime's cruelty and its close connection with cocaine pale by comparison with General Garcia-Meza's dictatorship. During his one year of rule (1980–1981), Garcia-Meza and his minister of the interior, Colonel Arce-Gomez, used the armed forces to assassinate protesting workers, torture dissidents, and abduct people suspected of conspiracy against the regime. Garcia-Meza operated with the assistance of Argentinean officers trained and proved at the Escuela de Mecánica de la Armada[47] (ESMA) in Buenos Aires, and his Nazi bent was demonstrated by the existence of the Novios de la Muerte ("Grooms of Death"), a paramilitary group from Santa Cruz that boasted swastikas and worshiped symbols of Hitler's Germany.[48] A prominent character who linked Garcia-Meza and cocaine magnate Roberto Suarez-Gomez was Klaus Altmann Barbie, whose extradition had been requested by France for the atrocities the Nazis had perpetrated in the city of Lyon when Barbie was the head of the Gestapo there.[49] In 1983 Barbie was handed over to France to be brought to trial.

In mid-1989, General Arrázola's arrest was reminiscent of the days of Garcia-Meza. Arrázola, commander of a Seventh Army division, was apprehended in the city of Cochabamba and charged with being involved with drug traffickers—he was still under arrest there in October 1990. The army division's connection with cocaine traffickers was not limited to Arrázola, however, and three highly ranked officers under his command managed to flee at the time of his arrest and were still at large in October 1990. Although no final decision as to Arrázola's responsibility had been made by October 1990, there was consensus among civilian and military observers that the general, who had represented García-Meza's regime before the trade unions,[50] was up to his ears in cocaine money. UMOPAR officers assert that what led to the general's arrest was the direct intervention of U.S. military attaché Colonel Hayes to have Arrázola investigated.[51]

Amid Latin America's move away from military regimes in the 1980s, the Bolivian generals were aware of the institutional risks presupposed by engaging in drug enforcement. General Jorge Moreira-Rojas, commander in chief of the armed forces, candidly alerted the administration and the citizenry in general that by persecuting cocaine dealers, the army would lose control over the officers who surrendered to the temptation of cocaine money. General Moreira declared that by engaging in drug enforcement, the army was running the risk of corruption.[52] A few months later, the head of the army, General Rolando Espinoza, conveyed the same fear: "If the President of the Republic, after the summit, decides to have us participate, we will do it for the sake of national security, despite the risks that this involves."[53]

The U.S. administration was not discouraged from urging Bolivia to engage its military in drug enforcement by the country's recent history of dictators and cocaine. Detailed information from the DEA and NAU in La Paz that General Arrázola's case was not an isolated one and that other army officers were entangled with traffickers was not dissuasive enough.[54] The weighty reasons for doubting the advantage of involving the army in the war on drugs did not prevent President Bush from pressing Bolivia, Peru, and Colombia into making a formal commitment in this direction.[55] After the Cartagena agreement, Presidents Bush and Paz-Zamora exchanged formal notes (known as Annex 3 of the Cartagena Accord) on May 9, 1990, in which they ratified their intent to accelerate the war on drugs in Bolivia by engaging the Bolivian Army. The purpose of militarizing enforcement is expressly mentioned in this annex, as the sum of $33,228,000 was allotted to drug enforcement in Bolivia, largely for army training and equipment.

At home, Paz-Zamora's pledge to the United States found staunch opposition from the coca growers and large political sectors. Peasant unions took a strong stand against the president's commitment; coca growers vowed through their leader, Evo Morales, to defend their plantations with their lives;[56] and the Senate dictated a formal resolution strongly disapproving of any sort of role for the army in drug policing.[57] In early April, nongovernment organizations in Bolivia expressed their support of the *cocaleros* by promising to stage a major campaign against the U.S.-backed militarization of drug enforcement,[58] arguing that engaging the army would critically escalate violations of human rights. In all likelihood, it was reasonably assumed, utilizing the army would increase the violence against the coca growers who were already enduring constant abuses from the UMOPAR.

Sectors of the Catholic church joined in denouncing the policy,[59] and the *cocaleros* also mustered international support. Forty-five legislators from fourteen Latin American countries held the fifth meeting of the Parlamento Latinoamericano in March 1990 and that body issued a statement repudiating the militarization of coca/cocaine enforcement. Such a step, the Parlamento stated, is a source of social instability.[60] In Bolivia, confining the armed forces to their institutional role within a civilian administration should not be imperiled by U.S. exigencies.[61] The previous twenty years of Bolivian history provided abundant data to support the efforts of Parlamento Latinoamericano, the nongovernmental human-rights organizations, and the peasant unions to keep the army out of the Chapare, but it was not just that history that spelled disaster; the separate interests of the army and the UMOPAR police in a struggling democracy were the key problems.

In response to the widespread concern, General Victor Vargas, commander of the airborne unit or brigade operating in the Chapare, hastened to calm the campesinos. Vargas assured them that the army posed no threat to coca growers and promised that the forces under his command were there to avert abuses on the part of other agencies,[62] an obvious allusion to the UMOPAR. Given the army's reputation, the general public must have found Vargas's pledge ridiculous.

Paz-Zamora's administration was also confronted with a legal aspect that further complicated the army's intervention. The 1988 antidrug law 1008 prescribes that a special council of cabinet ministers has the authority to dictate drug control policies.[63] Although the law foresees the armed forces' cooperation—in terms of personnel and equipment—at the request of the council,[64] procedural provisions confer the authority to conduct legal proceedings solely to the country's special forces.[65] Thus, the law has been construed as limiting the authority of the executive branch with regard to the army's intervention in drug enforcement.[66] The army may be called on to participate only if the police forces are overwhelmed by the drug traffic,[67] but even so, when it was suggested in April 1990 that they were being overpowered, there was an array of conflicting opinions from sectors within the Bolivian government.

The proposal to call in the army to cooperate with the UMOPAR could not surmount the objection that, according to the administration's claim, the country's 1990 antidrug achievements had substantially surpassed the previous year's accomplishments. Before meeting with President Bush in May 1990, President Paz-Zamora stated that calling the military into the war on drugs was unjustified because the police forces were faring well enough and the armed forces would cause "unnecessary violence."[68] The minister of the interior, Guillermo Capobianco, also stated that in spite of the UMOPAR's lack of equipment, neither Peru nor Colombia could match

Bolivia's accomplishments in drug enforcement.[69] In September, President Paz-Zamora went further and proudly declared that his country was controlling the drug business better than any other nation in the region.[70]

In May, Capobianco also stated flatly that the possibility that the UMOPAR would be defeated by the traffickers was more than remote, thus implying that there was no need to use the army for drug trade repression.[71] Raul Loaysa-Montoya, Capobianco's under-secretary and the person with direct authority over the Bolivian police forces, went further in his assessment of the situation and said that expectations about army intervention in the war were a stratagem of the political opposition.[72] Enforcement must be dealt with by the police, Loaysa staunchly said to me, and the chances that the UMOPAR might be overwhelmed by the traffickers were remote. Nonetheless, Loaysa added that although the Paz-Zamora administration was being effective in policing the cocaine business and in crop eradication, it was still a good idea to train army units just in case the drug business underwent an unforeseeable increase.[73]

At the U.S. Embassy, the prevailing opinion was at variance with that of President Paz-Zamora and his aides. As a signatory of the Cartagena Accord and the ensuing Annex 3, Bolivia is formally bound to engage its armed forces in the antidrug effort.[74] In September 1990, however, only Bolivia was still committed to engaging its army in antidrug operations as a last recourse.[75]

Besides the formal promise, there were strong practical considerations. It is true that Bolivia is not enduring the nightmare of the violent insurgency that plagues Colombia and Peru, but cocaine traffickers do exercise control over the remote region of Pando and a number of villages in the northern part of the Beni.[76] U.S. and Bolivian authorities are also worried about reports that in northwestern Pando, a region that borders the Peruvian and Brazilian Amazon, Shining Path is setting up encampments,[77] and La Paz newspapers tell how in the northern Beni cocaine magnates wanted by the authorities for drug offenses are able to walk around in broad daylight with no interference from the police.[78] Santa Ana de Yacuma and San Ramón are among the most striking cases, and U.S. Embassy officials' accounts of incidents reported in those localities suit the purpose of exerting pressure on the Bolivian government to engage the army there. Annex 3—the Embassy claims—prescribes that two light infantry regiments and an engineers' battalion operate in the Chapare and Beni regions and watch over the northern Peruvian border.[79]

THE POLITICAL DILEMMA

The issue of the army's intervention left Bolivian officials in a quandary. Politicians in power found it crucial to underline the Paz-Zamora administration's success in curbing the coca/cocaine business, but calling in the army would please the United States by exhibiting the staunchness required to reverse other Latin American countries' opinion about utilizing their military forces in such an effort. But calling in the army would also imply that things were not going that well after all. Clearly, praising the government's achievements, on the one hand, and escalating the war on drugs, on the other, are not compatible policies.

As revealed by a number of officials, large trafficking organizations remain intact and eradicated plots of coca have been replaced by others in more-inaccessible areas. Most experts on the drugs issue in Bolivia assert that the number of coca plots increased considerably in 1990,[80] and a Bolivian adviser to the DEA expressed his view that the official figures of the number of coca plots that have been eliminated do not reveal the real state of affairs. First, there is a considerable degree of deception in the accountancy of the eliminated areas; and second, new plantations in remote areas more than replace the lost *cocales* (coca plantations).[81] Furthermore, crop substitution in these new plantations is highly unlikely because the lack of roads in the region render the transportation and marketing of perishable products difficult if not impossible. Land that is suited to the growing of coca in the Chapare and Isiboro Secure regions alone exceeds 3 million hectars, which implies that for every parcel currently sown with coca, there are thirty other potential plots.

Deputy Under-Secretary of Social Defense Jorge Torrico has stated that despite the Paz-Zamora administration's "improvement" of the coca/cocaine situation, drug trafficking is surpassing the UMOPAR's capabilities.[82] This view indicates that this special police unit has its own shortcomings in providing solutions to the expansion of paste making and in reaching the upper echelons of the cocaine organizations.[83] These shortcomings, however, are at least partly a consequence of the UMOPAR's lack of adequate equipment and information.[84]

Besides equipment deficiencies, another development in 1990 also decreased the capability of the UMOPAR. The NAU office in La Paz decided it would be a good idea to turn the UMOPAR training course, Garras del Valor,[85] into an international event, and thus the U.S. Embassy dispatched joint U.S.-Bolivian invitations to European and Latin American governments to have their police forces send officers to be trained in that course in Chimoré.[86] The thinking was that the fifty-five-day training program in Chimoré would permit the international community to witness the professional capacities the Bolivian UMOPAR had acquired from its U.S. trainers,[87] but opening the course to foreign officers had visible disadvantages. For one thing, doing so shrank the number of UMOPAR personnel who could attend the course and squandered limited resources on foreign agents. Furthermore, the effort was a futile extravagance. Although the

Italians and Spaniards flatly turned down their invitations to participate in Garras del Valor, the members of German, Argentinean, and other police forces who did attend were baffled by the exotic environment in which the course was taught. In Argentina, drug enforcement has never taken place in the bush—as it does in countries where coca growing or cocaine manufacturing is carried out far from urban centers—and the European agents had never even seen such a setting let alone ever dreamed of operating in the jungle. It is no surprise that most of the guest trainees either did not start the course or did not complete it.[88] In short, resources were wasted at the expense of the UMOPAR for the sake of the image of the DEA/NAU and high Bolivian officers like General Felipe Carvajal.[89]

After the Cartagena summit in mid-February 1990, the United States stressed that the Americas demanded the contribution of the armies of the Southern Cone and that the State Department would fork over $33 million to Bolivia for war equipment, largely on the condition that the army be used in the war on drugs. The U.S. offer had a strong impact on the generals in Bolivia, and the view of the Bolivian military about its role in the war on drugs shifted dramatically. Abandoning the abstentious position they had held at Mar del Plata, Argentina, in 1987, those who participated in the discussions at the U.S. Embassy in La Paz took with them a long list of items that had caught their eye, as the U.S. expectations provided a unique opportunity to obtain these articles. Although many Bolivian observers believe the military were offered merely post–Korean War scrap,[90] the anachronism of the equipment did not disenchant the Bolivian military. One U.S. diplomatic official recalled his perplexity when the generals unrolled their inventory: "We were surprised that they did not demand submarines and aircraft-carriers," he said[91]—but, of course, Bolivia is a landlocked country.

Not everyone in the Bolivian military agreed with the government's resolution to engage the army in interdiction. Some high-ranking officers were skeptical, largely for three reasons. First, coordinating army action with that of the police had earlier posed insurmountable difficulties;[92] second, corruption is an everlasting danger for many officers; and third, army officers' nationalism could jeopardize the administration's endeavor to improve its relations with U.S. diplomats and enforcement officers deployed in Bolivia. Since late 1989, the Bolivian special forces had been under the unified command of a retired and reputable army general named Lucio Añez, and in October 1990,[93] General Añez did not have the slightest confidence that once into the war on drugs, the army would be any safer from the economic temptations of cocaine than UMOPAR agents. Harmony between the military and the UMOPAR at this stage was also so unlikely[94] that the possibility of their cooperating seemed almost impossible.

There appeared to be three equally nonviable alternatives for action coordination. First, each force might operate independently, an option that all the parties considered inadmissable because it would mean interforce conflict and inefficiency. Second, the joint command might be unified under the control of army officers, but the UMOPAR found this option intolerable. President Paz-Zamora had ordered the army to support the UMOPAR with intelligence and logistics, a secondary role,[95] and the UMOPAR believed that since its agents were the ones who had been risking their skin in the jungle, it should have a central role. Third, unified leadership might be given to the UMOPAR, but the armed forces found this option insufferable. The military had traditionally viewed the police as being less important, historically relegated to lesser matters than defending the country's sovereignty. This view was clearly laid out by Marcelo Quiroga-Obregon, a member of the Chamber of Deputies Defense Commission, when he rejected the possibility of subordinating the armed forces to the UMOPAR because the former "were born before the Republic and represent the country's fundamental custodian which cannot therefore be subordinated to any other institution than the constitution."[96]

The military's contempt for the police has a long history in Bolivia, and it turned into hatred in 1952 when the junta of General Ballivián was toppled by the Paz-Estenssoro revolution. The generals are still unable to forget that the police force not only supported Paz-Estenssoro against the army's regime but also ventured to close down the military academy.[97] The events of 1952 were viewed by the army as a challenge to its esprit de corps, and in 1990, the issue of joining with the UMOPAR in drug enforcement opened old scars.

The New War: The Army Versus the Police

When the interim commander in chief of the army, General Guido Sandoval, stated that the armed forces were ready to "broaden" antidrug operations, then limited almost entirely to the police, it was clear that trouble over institutional hegemony had emerged. The chief of the UMOPAR, General Felipe Carvajal, reacted briskly by bringing the army down to size. Voicing his force's conviction, Carvajal announced publicly that the army would have to subordinate its job to that of the UMOPAR,[98] explaining that the experience and technical skills of his force demanded that the army make do with a secondary role in drug enforcement.[99] Seemingly, there was no way to even minimally satisfy the aspirations of both the army and the UMOPAR.

In early April 1990, President Paz-Zamora ordered the Barrientos and Ustariz infantry regiments to get ready to fight the cocaine traffic in the Chapare jungle, and soon thereafter, the commanding officer of the Barrientos unit, Colonel Rodriguez, conveyed to civilians in Cochabamba that once joint drug enforcement operations had started, the first task of the army would be to crack down on the UMOPAR and the DEA. According to the colonel, the UMOPAR deserved to be dismantled given its twofold contamination: A large sector of the UMOPAR had been bought off by the traffickers, and the entire force had sold its loyalty to the DEA *Yankis,* a bunch of corrupt interlopers.[100] From other similar declarations recorded at that time, foreign intelligence in La Paz found that Colonel Rodriguez had not spoken out of personal eccentricity and that his opinion was shared by many of his comrades.[101]

The army's declared animosity against the UMOPAR and the DEA proved to be serious. In addition to a series of minor hostile incidents between the army and the UMOPAR, the army also demonstrated a stated lack of sympathy for the DEA. Officers from the Barrientos regiment, which is situated on the road from the town of Cochabamba to the Chapare, arrested three DEA agents on the grounds that the men were not carrying adequate personal credentials,[102] an act the U.S. Embassy considered exasperating given the diplomatic status of the DEA personnel.

After the Barrientos infantry regiment began maneuvers in the Chapare, to pose a "dissuasive, psychological obstacle" to traffickers,[103] a landmark in the history of friction between the army and the police occurred. On May 7, a group of young army officers attacked four UMOPAR agents near their barracks in Villa Tunari. After suffering threats and provocations from a dozen troopers from the Barrientos regiment at a canteen near Villa Tunari, three of the UMOPAR agents managed to escape. The fourth, however, a corporal named Pedro Mariani,[104] was caught by the tormentors after unsuccessfully attempting to hide in his girl friend's room at the back of the canteen. A brief description of circumstances surrounding the beating of Corporal Mariani indicates, not a personal feud, but institutional incompatibility. Mariani was severely battered and later driven away to the Barrientos regiment's bivouac. There he was repeatedly beaten almost to death. On May 11, UMOPAR Captain Mario Ayala was called from the Barrientos regiment to take the corporal back to his unit. In view of the painful state the corporal was in, the captain demanded that a written report be signed by military officers with a description of Mariani's physical condition. Ayala wanted to avoid the responsibility in the event the corporal did not make it to the hospital alive.[105]

After being flown from the Chapare to the city of Cochabamba, Mariani was in the intensive care unit for five days, and even at the end of May, he was still convalescing, and showing physical signs of the incident. The military personnel who had beaten Mariani explained to the army colonel in charge of probing the episode that the victim had been trying to take photographs of them, but even this frail attempt to justify the aggression was thwarted by eyewitnesses who declared that the battered corporal was not carrying a camera. The investigation itself brought about further complaints from UMOPAR personnel. Interrogated by army officers conducting the probe, the UMOPAR agents complained of being inquisitorially dealt with during the investigation, maintaining that they were treated by the colonel and his staff as suspects instead of witnesses.[106]

In the aftermath of the Mariani incident, the commander in chief of the army declared that the episode had not altered the "normal activities of both forces,"[107] but UMOPAR officers did not agree with this statement, as the brisk response of the head of the Garras del Valor course demonstrates. In response to the top army commander's statement, UMOPAR Captain Ayala asserted that "future provocations" from the army would bring about "unwavering retaliation" from the UMOPAR.[108] This response was not issued by a formal spokesman for the UMOPAR, nor did it have the appropriate style required to ease the interforce conflict, but it did make clear that underneath the Mariani incident there was a deeper confrontation. Interagency friction is likely to neutralize any attempt to attain an acceptable degree of cooperation between the UMOPAR and the armed forces, and by mid-May, the pessimistic forecast that cooperation between the army and the police would not work had proved to be correct. Two other events demonstrate the point.

In May 1990, the second in command of the UMOPAR Chapare outpost at Chimoré was Major Ramiro Ortega, and through an internal memorandum, he reported another perplexing incident to the commander of the Bolivian special forces, General Añez. The memorandum said that on May 10, at 10 A.M., "army personnel opened fire on our helicopters to deter them from flying above their encampment. To avoid a confrontation, we immediately flew away."[109] As the head of the antidrug forces, General Añez notified his colleague, commander in chief of the army, General Moreira, who tried to downplay the report as if nothing serious had happened. To quell the gravity of the accusation and calm public opinion, General Moreira attributed the indictment to the "hypersensitivity of the UMOPAR."[110] It is unlikely that Moreira's statement had a diluting effect on those concerned about the dispute, and in political circles, his reply was interpreted as being unduly nonchalant.

Also in May 1990, a bloody occurrence in the Chapare village of Isinuta raised suspicions of further army aggression against the UMOPAR. A hand grenade hurled at a UMOPAR officer sitting at a bar killed the agent and four civilians, including a four-year old, and also wounded several bystanders.[111] The assassin was found drunk a few hours later by an enraged mob who burned him to death. The man was a well-known desperado with links to traffickers from Santa Cruz, and the incident could have passed as an inconsequential felony, however horrifying, committed from sheer lunacy. But UMOPAR officers and regular-policemen conducting the investigation grew increasingly suspicious that the military stationed in the Chapare had been behind the event, as examination of the grenade shrapnel indicated that the explosive was of the type that only the army has access to.[112] The purpose of the criminal onslaught, UMOPAR personnel in the Chapare conjectured, was to demonstrate that the UMOPAR is unable to control the situation and thus compel army intervention.

In spite of the origin of the grenade, it is possible that the suspicion that military officers were involved in the multiple murder is not solidly grounded. However, after the awkward Mariani and helicopters affairs, there is plenty of reason to justify the UMOPAR's misgivings. When I left the Chapare at the end of May 1990, there was a general conviction among the UMOPAR agents that from then on, they would have to safeguard themselves from treachery that soldiers from the Barrientos or the Ustariz could unleash.[113] This grim picture of the joint UMOPAR-army endeavor was attributed by several politicians to the U.S. Embassy. One Bolivian congressman, Gregorio Lanza, claimed that Americans in Bolivia brought about—and also set the pace—of the UMOPAR-army confrontation by urging the policy of military intervention, pushing that policy in Bolivia, and usurping such decisions as which regiments to deploy, how many forces to commission, and what they are to do.[114]

5. SOME CONCLUSIONS

The case of "who is cheating on whom," concerning the missing 156 hectares, may not appear as clearly paradoxical as the events described in the other two sections, but three paradoxical aspects of the missing 156-hectare case are significant. First, the episode shows that the Bolivians' cheating to their own advantage benefited more than the Bolivian officials who ordered and performed the forgery and even Bolivia itself; the officials sent by the United States to control the eradication procedures also benefited from the fabrication. Bolivian and U.S. personnel seem to have reached some informal and tacit understanding whereby the former appeared to be carrying out their commitment and the latter seemed to be doing their part in promoting coca eradication in Bolivia. Such an understanding distorts the very role of the U.S. personnel whose job is, among other things, to supervise the Bolivians.

The second paradoxical aspect concerns the promotion of DIRECO's chief, Zamendo, allegedly the perpetrator of the forgery, to a position in the U.S. Embassy to exercise control over eradication. Zamendo not only got away with at least overlooking the fabrication but was rewarded with a promotion in status and a better wage. The third aspect relates to the morale of native and foreign personnel concerned with the coca/cocaine issue. Since the episode, few officials will take figures disclosed by either the government or U.S. officials in Bolivia as serious indicators of what is actually going on. I explain the logic of the 156-hectare event in Chapter 5.

When NAU officials explained that no forgery was possible because of the existence of officers to control the eradication process,[115] one is inclined to think that the fox is taking care of the chickens. Awards were granted to people who disobeyed the rules, and those who obeyed the rules were demoted. In other words, the people responsible for the forgery were commissioned to watch out for future deception. There is also the odd way U.S. and Bolivian officials reached a way to understand each other and thus minimize personal friction. This topic, too, is dealt with in Chapter 5.

Paradoxical behavior is obvious in the section "If You Want to Succeed, Avoid Success." As interpreted by the bureaucrats in charge, two "reasonable" instructions issued for the furtherance of the same goal are rendered incompatible. "Beat drug trafficking by making the business unprofitable" appears to exclude "apprehend transgressors and seize their cocaine and necessary materials to diminish the drug traffic." Although there is no logical contradiction between these two commands, because an obvious way to bring down prices is to make arrests and seizures, the way these injunctions have been construed by the bureaucrats has created a paradox. Research has shown that the UMOPAR efforts to arrest traffickers and harass coca stompers and cocaine brokers resulted in the slump of prices in the Chapare. Transactions decreased and so did the opportunities for performing arrests and seizures, and U.S. officials threatened to impose a penalty upon the UMOPAR for failing to capture dealers.[116] Had the UMOPAR arrested more traffickers instead, the complaint would have consisted of their not having discouraged the trade. There is no way to win without losing.

In the section dealing with bringing in the army, two main paradoxes are immediately apparent. The first originates in the tortuous path the Bolivian administration had to take to be able to call in the army; the second consists of the negative consequences of adding more resources to fight the war on drugs. Legal rules and the need to distinguish between enforcement and defense functions—and the special purpose of police agencies to deal with those rules—made it difficult for the government to justify its commitment to the United States. The distinction between police and military duties has a special weight in Latin America as a consequence of the "dirty wars" against "subversive" campaigns in the 1960s and 1970s in Brazil, Uruguay, Argentina, and Chile and today in Colombia, Peru, and Central America.

To give in to the pressure exerted on the Bolivian government by the United States to have Bolivia's armed forces fight cocaine trafficking would not only please the United States but also demonstrate Bolivia's determination. By calling the army in, Paz-Zamora would portray a resolution to take the bull by the horns that the preceding governments did not display. But such a resolution would involve a new dilemma. The government would have to face the option of, one, appearing to have failed to control drug trafficking in order to justify the army's intervention, and thus convey a poor image of enforcement efficiency until April 1990; or, two, claiming to have been successful, in which case there would be no reason to "militarize" enforcement. "Doing well" at enforcement and "doing well" in opting for the U.S.-backed policy of calling the army in are blatantly contradictory. The opinions of the above-mentioned officials were closely related to their positions in their various bureaucracies. Officials in command of the police gloated over their success; among the rest, positions varied sharply.

Finally, what seems to be an increase in the use of power to control the cocaine trade has so far resulted in the opposite situation. Being a new, well-defined interest group in the war on drugs, the army has collided with the UMOPAR and the DEA. The military's first steps in the Chapare brought about clashes with the Leopardos and then open quarrels among the upper cadres of the forces. Conflict took the place of cooperation.[117]

I have so far depicted the way in which confrontation arises among peasants and between peasants and Cambas (Chapter 1) and among enforcement agents (Chapters 2, 3, and 4). In Chapter 5, I develop an explanation for these conflicting situations, particularly those concerning enforcement agencies, as well as analyze the way in which Bolivian and U.S. bureaucracies resolve their own conflicts.

NOTES

1. Paul Watzlawick, Janet Beavin, and Don D. Jackson, *Teoria de la comunicacion humana: Interacciones, patologias y paradojas*, translated from English by Carlos E. Sluzki, 3d ed. (Buenos Aires, Argentina: Editorial Tiempo Contemporaneo, 1974), Chapter 6.

2. In Chapter 5, section 1, I distinguish between "policy paradoxes" and "bureaucratic paradoxes."

3. See Guillermo Bedregal-Gutierrez and Ruddy Viscarra-Pando, *La lucha boliviana contra el narcotrafico* (La Paz: Los Amigos del Libro, 1989), Chapters 4 and 5.

4. PIDYS stands for Integral Project of Development and Substitution (of coca crops).

5. See Bedregal-Gutierrez and Viscarra-Pando, *La lucha boliviana*, p. 142.

6. DIRECO (Dirección de Reconversion de la Coca) is a technical institution of engineers, rural technicians, agricultural experts, etc.

7. Interview with a high DIRECO official, Villa Tunari, May 26, 1990.

8. Interviews with two U.S. Embassy officials in La Paz on May 23 and 24, 1990.

9. Interview with a NAU officer in the Chapare, May 27, 1990.

10. Some witnesses assert it was Aguilar in person who came up with the proposal.

11. Interview with a NAU official in Cochabamba, January 14, 1990.

12. INM is the Washington D.C.–based International Narcotic Matters, which runs the NAU agencies deployed overseas. INM operates within the jurisdiction of the State Department.

13. *Ultima Hora* (La Paz), January 20, 1990.

14. Interview with a NAU officer, May 28, 1990.

15. Interview with a researcher working for SIRES, a prestigious institute in Cochabamba, May 27, 1990. For a short discussion of General Garcia-Meza's dictatorship, see section 4 of this chapter.

16. Interview in Cochabamba with researchers at the SIRES institute, May 27, 1990.

17. Interview with two UMOPAR officers in Chimoré, May 29, 1990.

18. Interview at the under-secretary's office in La Paz, May 25, 1990.

19. Interview at his office, May 22, 1990. The under-secretary of social defense serves under the jurisdiction of the minister of the interior.

20. See INM report of April 1990.

21. A *carga* is equivalent to 45 kilos (100 pounds).

22. Interview at the U.S. Embassy, May 24, 1990.

23. Interviews with two U.S. Embassy officials on May 23 and 24, 1990.

24. One of these disbelievers was Armando Aquino-Huerta, a Bolivian lawyer and DEA adviser who had served as a special prosecutor for drug matters (interview at his office in La Paz, May 24, 1990).

25. I got this impression from embassy adviser and former DEA agent, Julian Lindenauer (interview at the Plaza Hotel in La Paz, May 22, 1990).

26. Interview occurred on a plot that belongs to Eudoro Barrientos, a prominent local *cocalero* union leader. Villanueva is supposed to have rid itself of coca dependence (Roger N. Rasnake and Michael Painter, *Rural Development and Crop Substitution in Bolivia: USAID and the Chapare Development Project*, Cooperative Agreement on Human Settlements and Natural Resource System [Institute for Development Anthropology, Clark University, Worcester, Massachusetts, and Institute for Development Anthropology, Binghamton, New York, 1989], p. 20), but on May 29, I was able to see endless new *cocales* near Barrientos's plot.

27. The village is also called Eteramazama.

28. Interview with a NAU agent in Villa Tunari, May 28, 1990; also another with an UMOPAR officer, Chimoré, May 29, 1990.

29. This was the declared goal of both Operation Blast Furnace in 1986 (see Chapter 2, section 2) and the Cartagena Agreement signed on February 15, 1990.

30. Interview with a NAU officer, U.S. Embassy, May 24, 1990.

31. See unsigned editorial note, "Los ejercitos frente a la droga," *Nueva Sociedad* (Caracas) (July-August 1989), p. 136. See also Steven Wisotsky, *Beyond the War on Drugs: Overcoming a Failed Public Policy* (Buffalo, N.Y.: Prometheus Books, 1990), p. 162.

32. I take the license of overlooking the case of Paraguay, a country where elections are almost universally considered rigged. In dealing with the generals as President Raúl Alfonsin's senior adviser on human rights and institutional affairs, I was aware of the prevailing opinion on the issue. Information about the meeting was supplied to me by Alfonsin's secretary of defense, Adalberto Rodriguez-Giavarini, Buenos Aires, September 29, 1989.

33. Ibid.

34. Interviews with Adalberto Rodriguez-Giavarini, Buenos Aires, July 9, 1989, and September 22, 1989.

35. In Annex 3 of the Cartagena Accord signed by Presidents Bush and Paz-Zamora in May 1990 to complement the multilateral agreement among Colombia, Peru, Bolivia, and the United States, it is expressly stated that drug trafficking poses a threat to the internal security of Bolivia.

36. Mexico's president, Carlos Salinas-Gortari turned the drug issue into one of national security (*New York Times*, December 12, 1988).

37. See Donald Mabry, "The US Military and the War on Drugs in Latin America," *Journal of Interamerican Studies and World Affairs* 30:2–3 (Summer/Fall 1988), p. 53.

38. Ibid. The issue was discussed at length by the Association of the Bar of the City of New York, Committees of Lectures and Continuing Education and Military Affairs and Justice, "Using the Military to Fight Drugs: All Right or All Wrong?" April 18, 1990 (I was on the panel).

39. Since January 1990, Hugo Cochamanidis has been the director of the Bolivian Dirección Nacional de la Coca. In an interview on May 24, 1990, he recalled the army's poor record concerning the coca/cocaine issue.

40. See Chapter 3, section 3.

41. Ibid.

42. See Chapter 1, section 3.

43. James Dunkerley, *Rebellion in the Veins: Political Struggle in Bolivia 1952–1982* (London: Verso, 1984), p. 201.

44. See June Nash, *We Eat the Mines and the Mines Eat Us* (New York: Columbia University, 1979); and Dunkerley, *Rebellion in the Veins*, Chapter 6.

45. Dunkerley, *Rebellion in the Veins*, p. 318.

46. Ibid.

47. For detailed descriptions of what went on at the Escuela de Mecánica de la Armada in Buenos Aires from 1976 on, see Informe de la Comision Nacional Sobre la Desaparicion de Personas, *Nunca Mas* (Buenos Aires: Editorial Universitaria, 1986), p. 80, and Iain Guest, *Behind the Disappearances* (Philadelphia: University of Pennsylvania Press, 1990), Chapter 1.

48. It seems this group was still active in the 1990s (interview with Enrique Valverde, head of the Narcotics Assistance Unit [NAU] in Cochabamba and a NAU adviser, Cochabamba, May 26, 1990).

49. Enrique Valverde had the opportunity in his youth to hear Barbie speak of the Nazi era with nostalgia (interview held on May 26, 1990).

50. In 1981, in an attempt to appease the bellicose miners unions, the then-Colonel Arrázola had promised to release political prisoners and to guarantee workers a minimal stability in their jobs. Considering the agreement to be too benevolent, the government did not honor it (Dunkerley, *Rebellion in the Veins*, p. 296).

51. Statements made to me by an UMOPAR captain in Villa Tunari, May 26, 1990.

52. *Ultima Hora*, January 16, 1990.

53. *Ultima Hora*, February 3, 1990.

54. The NAU had made a full report to its headquarters in La Paz (statement of a NAU official who had participated in writing the report in an interview, October 4, 1990).

55. The U.S. administration's resolution to have these countries' armies involved in drug enforcement is specified in the White House, National Drug Control Strategy (Washington, D.C.: U.S. Govt. Printing Office, January 1990). This report states that increasing "the effectiveness of law enforcement and military activities in the three countries against cocaine trade" is one of the main goals (p. 50).

56. *Ultima Hora*, April 4, 1990; also *Presencia* (La Paz), May 9, 1990.

57. *Ultima Hora*, January 16, 1990.

58. *Presencia*, April 8, 1990.

59. As an indication of the church's concern about the rights of the peasants being trampled upon by the army, see Dunkerley, *Rebellion in the Veins*, p. 215.

60. See *Presencia* and *Ultima Hora*, March 21, 1990.

61. See an unsigned article, "Militarizacion versus democracia," in *Presencia*, March 17, 1990. Also see U.S. Congress, Committee on Government Operations, "Thirty-Eighth Report: United States Anti-Narcotics Activities in the Andean Region," (Washington, D.C.: August 30, 1990), p. 77.

62. *Opinion* (Cochabamba), April 15, 1990.

63. The Consejo Nacional del Trafico Ilicito y Uso Indebido de Drogas (CONALID, National Council for Illicit Traffic and Undue Consumption of Drugs), created by law 1008 in July 1988, is integrated with the ministries of Foreign Affairs, Justice and the Interior, Coordination and Planning, Public Health, Defense, Finance, and Aeronautics (article 133). CONALID has supreme authority over the special forces, and is entitled to appeal to the armed forces for personnel and equipment (law 1008, article 135). Until May 1990, these special forces consisted of narcotics (urban) police, UMOPAR police, air force pilots, and naval officers operating under the unified command of a retired army general (see Chapter 2, section 3).

64. Law 1008, article 135.

65. Article 85(a) of law 1008 prescribes that the special force will initiate the proceedings in drug-related cases. Article 86 abbreviates the procedure and

establishes the auxiliary role of the police. Similarly, article 92(a) stipulates that special prosecutors have authority over the police forces.

66. This intervention was foreseen in law 1008, article 135.

67. Such an interpretation is compatible with Annex 3 of the Cartagena Accord, in which it is stated that repression of drug trafficking is essentially a police matter.

68. *Ultima Hora*, May 8, 1990.

69. *Ultima Hora*, May 9, 1990.

70. "I do not know where the ambassador may have gotten the information from. Bolivia has proved to be the first country in fighting narco-traffic in Latin America and has beaten all records of efficiency in that terrain" (President Paz-Zamora, in response to public complaints from U.S. Ambassador Robert Gelbard; *La Razon* [La Paz], September 27, 1990).

71. *Ultima Hora*, May 23, 1990.

72. Interview at the Ministry of the Interior, May 25, 1990.

73. Ibid.

74. Clause II-B of Annex 3 of the Cartagena Accord; see *Ultima Hora*, April 29, 1990.

75. Presidents Alberto Fujimori of Peru and Cesar Gaviria-Trujillo of Colombia—both having assumed office after the accord was signed—staunchly opposed such involvement. In the opinion of President Gaviria, "demilitarizing" drug enforcement, in spite of military claims of considerable success, is necessary to reduce out-of-control violence (*Buenos Aires Herald*, September 16, 1990). However, giving in to State Department pressure, in January 1991 Fujimori changed his stance and committed himself to ordering the army into the Huallaga Valley.

76. U.S. Ambassador Robert Gelbard conveyed his concern about this presence to me in an interview held at the U.S. Embassy, La Paz, on September 13, 1989.

77. Today, NAU officials confess that U.S. forces, the DEA in particular, would not dare to deal with cocaine operations known to take place in that area (interview with a U.S. Embassy official, La Paz, October 6, 1990).

78. See *Ultima Hora*, February 17, 1990; also, Wisotsky, *Beyond the War on Drugs*, p. 157.

79. Annex 3, Section II(D.1.a). Interview with a high NAU official at the U.S. Embassy, May 24, 1990.

80. Interview with Doctor Armando Aquino-Huerta, adviser to the DEA in Bolivia, at his office in La Paz, May 24, 1990.

81. Ibid.

82. Interview with Torrico in La Paz, May 22, 1990.

83. Interviews with NAU agent Gustavo Araujo in Cochabamba and UMOPAR Captain Mario Ayala in Chimoré May 29, 1990.

84. I have already explained the connection between the UMOPAR's lack of equipment and the army's vetoing each attempt made by the U.S. Embassy to supply modern arms and communication gear to the UMOPAR (see Chapter 2, section 3). See also Manuel Benitez-Larroca, "UMOPAR libra una batalla desigual contra el narcotráfico en Chapare," *Presencia*, March 18, 1990.

85. Garras del Valor translates as "Clutches of Valor."

86. According to *Presencia* (January 27, 1990), the invitations were issued by NAU's top official at the U.S. Embassy, Brian Stickney, and General Felipe Carvajal, commander of the Bolivian police force.

87. The complaint that UMOPAR did not have sufficient ammunition, uniforms, mattresses, and so forth did not apply to the Garras del Valor course. Officers in this program have not endured any such shortages (interviews with UMOPAR Captain Mario Ayala and NAU agent Gustavo, interviews in Chimoré, May 29, 1990).

88. Interviews with NAU agent Gustavo A. and UMOPAR Captain Mario Ayala, May 29, 1990, and Enrique Valverde, Villa Tunari, May 30, 1990.

89. UMOPAR and NAU officers in the Chapare believe that the idea came from top NAU agents in La Paz (interviews conducted in the Chapare May 27–30, 1990).

90. Interviews with Hugo Cochamanidis, La Paz, May 24, 1990, and Bolivian congressman Ernesto Machicado, La Paz, May 25, 1990.

91. Interview with an official of the U.S. Embassy who asked not to be named, May 23, 1990.

92. See Operation Blast Furnace (Chapter 2, section 2).

93. According to a top Federal Police officer at the Superintendencia de Drogas Peligrosas in Buenos Aires, General Añez had a reputation for his personal decency and democratic convictions (interview with the head of the bureau, Comisario General Raul Armesto, July 11, 1990).

94. Interview with General Lucio Añez, May 31, 1990.

95. Samuel Doria-Medina, Bolivian presidential adviser, added that the army's role should be confined to contributing to the building of an infrastructure to facilitate the implementation of an alternative development plan (*Presencia*, March 16, 1990). This view is widely shared by scholars and politicians in Bolivia today.

96. *Ultima Hora*, April 4, 1990. Seemingly, Quiroga-Obregon overlooked the fact that the democratically elected president is the constitutional commander of the armed forces.

97. For an account of these developments see Dunkerley, *Rebellion in the Veins*, Chapter 1.

98. *Ultima Hora*, March 21, 1990.

99. *Ultima Hora*, May 31, 1990.

100. Opinion voiced to Enrique Valverde, former head of the NAU in Cochabamba, by a high military source. The source was not identified (interview with Valverde in the Chapare village of Irvirgarzama, May 26, 1990).

101. Interview with an Argentinean intelligence agent in Bolivia, May 21, 1990.

102. Interview with an UMOPAR officer in Cochabamba, May 25, 1990, and Enrique Valverde, May 26, 1990.

103. The commander of the airborne brigade, General Victor Vargas, declared that the presence of the army posed a psychological deterrent to the traffickers. The army's salient role in protecting the "internal order" also safeguarded the peasantry from alleged abuses from the UMOPAR (*Opinion*, April 15, 1990).

104. Some versions refer to the corporal as Mamani.

105. Interview with UMOPAR Captain Ayala in Chimoré, May 29, 1990. Enrique Valverde agreed with Ayala's version (interview on May 29, 1990).

106. Interview with an UMOPAR noncommissioned officer, Chimoré, May 29, 1990.
107. *Presencia*, May 16, 1990.
108. Ibid.
109. ANF news agency in La Paz, May 17, 1990.
110. *Ultima Hora*, May 22, 1990.
111. Interview with a regular police officer investigating the case, Villa Tunari, May 29, 1990, and a conversation with Enrique Valverde, May 30, 1990.
112. An oral report was submitted on May 28, 1990, to one of the top officers in the Chimoré training course Garras del Valor by a regular-police officer commissioned to probe the incident. I was present at that meeting.
113. Conversation with NAU agent Gustavo A. and the police officer conducting the investigation, Villa Tunari, May 31, 1990.
114. See Gregorio Lanza, "Policia, Fuerzas Armadas, y trafico de drogas," *Presencia*, April 28, 1990, p. 8.
115. Meeting at the U.S. Embassy on May 24, 1990.
116. Whether withdrawing the bonus is actually a threat or just the deprivation of an advantage is controversial. Whatever the label, the measure is clearly coercive. The $50 bonus creates a "floor" of minimal relief, and its loss would imply serious deprivation to UMOPAR agents so that possibility reduces their options. For an analysis of this issue see Michael Taylor, *Community, Anarchy, and Liberty* (Cambridge: Cambridge University Press, 1982), Chapter 1, and Alan Wertheimer, *Coercion* (Princeton: Princeton University Press, 1989), p. 204.
117. Having the military join the antidrug campaign in Bolivia means more than bringing the armed forces back into the center of the political scenario. As correctly pointed out by Louis Goodman and Johanna S. R. Mendelson ("The Threat of New Missions: Latin American Militaries and the Drug War," in *The Military and Democracy: The Future of Civil-Military Relations in Latin America*, ed. Louis Goodman et al., [Lexington Mass. and Toronto: Lexington Books, 1990], p. 189), the negative effects of military intervention have much broader consequences.

5

In the Realm of Paradoxes

Bolivia has made a remarkable transitioning this decade from a trafficker-influenced military regime to democratic government with a coca eradication program. Our certification decision is based on the fact that the 1988 record is the best annual performance to date. Bolivia passed and implemented a strong anti-narcotics law during 1988. Leading trafficker Roberto Suarez was arrested and remains in prison. Bolivia exceeded the 1,800 hectare eradication target spelled out in our bilateral narcotic agreement signed in 1987 and began forcible eradication. Interdiction efforts were improved leading to a sharp increase in the number of drug seizures. In addition the riverine interdiction program, problematic throughout the year, appears back on track with the government of Bolivia's appointment of a new, highly professional navy commander in December. However, despite these efforts, total coca cultivation continued to increase and high prices for coca leaf are hurting the voluntary eradication program. In sum, we think Bolivia made a good effort in 1988, but increased production is particularly worrisome and more must be done to deter the spread of coca cultivation.
—International Narcotics Control: The President's March 1, 1989, Certification for Foreign Assistance Eligibility and Options for Congressional Action

1. A FRESH START

In 1990, coca/cocaine control in Bolivia seemed to have reached a point of equilibrium, and facts strongly suggest that, other things being equal, the bureaucracies involved in coca eradication and coca/cocaine interdiction would perpetuate that situation. Although minor shifts may take place, there are grounds to assume that, in essence, the joint U.S.-Bolivian enforcement strategy is doomed to keep on failing. Beyond the war on drugs rhetoric adopted by the U.S. and Bolivian administrations, there are powerful reasons for both countries to pursue the elimination of the cocaine business. It is widely accepted that the annihilation of coca crops and cocaine trafficking in Bolivia would mean a significant reduction of the flow of cocaine into the United States from one of its major sources, and Bolivia has good reasons to work with the United States in striving to rid itself of the drug business. It is clear that the coca/cocaine economy hinders economic growth, contaminates the official bureaucracy with drug money, and challenges the power of an already extremely weak state.[1]

A substitute economy is likely to alleviate Bolivia's endemic poverty for two reasons: First, it may be presumed that a substitute for the coca/cocaine economy would recycle a larger portion of the new industry's gains into the country's market, which would foster investment and thus alleviate Bolivia's chronic unemployment; second, it may reasonably be expected that the state would control such an economy and thus be able to tax its revenues, which would enable a distribution of wealth that would eliminate extreme poverty. A new economy based on cotton, tin, or tropical fruits is likely to promote the country's general interest and even the interests of those sectors that are currently devoted to the coca/cocaine industry. According to experts and peasant union leaders, a large portion of the coca growers would gladly relinquish a portion of their meager earnings in order to avoid the risks they currently face every day.[2] It is not true, therefore, as is often claimed, that only increased profits will drive peasants away from the Chapare's coca/cocaine industry.

The repressive campaign that resulted from the war on drugs conception has systematically frustrated expectations that the strategy would lead Americans and Bolivians in the direction of reducing cocaine manufacturing and trafficking.[3] To deal with the paradoxes the repressive U.S.-Bolivian antidrug campaign has effected, distortions of the strategy must be tackled on two levels: first, on the level of the bureaucratic apparatus involved in the war and, second, on the level of the individual people who are devoted to the anticocaine campaign. An analysis of a third level, which concerns drug control within the context of U.S. global policies, surpasses the purpose of this book and will not be discussed. By this general political level, I mean the political motivations and choices, such as the underlying reasons for the war on drugs approach itself and how the drug problem and other competing interests governing U.S. foreign relations are traded off.[4]

Although this book does not specifically focus on Bolivia's politics and economy, the drug enforcement's shortcomings have been described against the background of the country's institutional and financial plight. Bolivian officials of all ranks know that uprooting the cocaine trade will bring about unbearable side effects in the short and medium term unless unforeseen economic transformations enable the country to mobilize national resources and absorb a mass of coca/cocaine business layoffs.[5] As things stand, victory over coca/cocaine manufacturing and traffic would cause dreadful consequences in the forms of extreme recession and unprecedented unemployment. U.S. Embassy officials acknowledge that if successful, repression of the drug traffic may generate an invasion of the largest urban centers and, consequently, uncontrollable social unrest and a sharp increase in urban criminality.[6] Trade unions could bring the country to a complete standstill in a last desperate attempt to protect the coca growers, their strongest clientele since the virtual disappearance of the mining industry.[7] Bolivia's policy options and solutions are, however, far beyond the reach of this book.

I wish to discuss two points that flow from the preceding chapters: First, outcomes that contradict the primary purposes of the antidrug campaign in Bolivia result from the behavior of bureaucrats who are committed to coca/cocaine enforcement and eradication; second, U.S. and Bolivian bureaucrats are similar in their proneness to contravene both countries' general interests as these interests have been officially spelled out. Both of these points are valid both with respect to the anti-coca/cocaine agencies and with respect to individuals within those agencies.

For the purpose of this analysis, I differentiate two sorts of paradoxes: "policy paradoxes" and "bureaucratic paradoxes."[8] The first class consists of results of political strategies that contradict the goals pursued by the strategies themselves. An example of a policy paradox is the increase in drug manufacturing as a consequence of enforcement.[9] Bureaucratic paradoxes, with which this chapter is basically concerned, are incongruities generated within the state apparatus, as contradictions emerge between formal attempts to advance the general interest and the pursuance of interests of either bureaucratic agencies[10] or officials operating within those agencies. Such paradoxes appear throughout this book (especially in Chapter 4) and reflect, first, that overgrown antidrug bureaucracies generate insurmountable contradictions and, second, that, in the case of Bolivia and the United States, paradoxical behavior has become a part of both countries' actions.

2. BUREAUCRACIES AT WORK

The NAU and the DEA have become dominant agencies in U.S. foreign policy since the drug issue came to the top of the U.S. political agenda, namely, as a threat to U.S. national security.[11] NAU and DEA agents are being deployed throughout the world to administer vast resources, and they are mustering sizable political clout in the countries in which they operate. NAU and DEA personnel wield a decisive weight in international policymaking, and their reports have considerable bearing on setting priorities in U.S. foreign policy, especially with regard to Latin America[12] and Asia.

Overseas, U.S. personnel enjoy diplomatic immunities, special bonuses, and wage supplements for what are broadly considered risky tasks. They have plenty of time off, and in Bolivia, they spend it in the most luxurious hotels. In 1986, when Operation Blast Furnace was being staged,[13] one of the top U.S. military officers assigned to Bolivia could not be reached at one point because, allegedly, this officer was playing golf in Panama.[14] It is no wonder that the NAU and DEA have intensified the pursuance of their sectorial interests;[15] it is worthwhile preserving a situation in which the good life thrives.[16]

An example of such a pursuance concerns the February 1990 slump in the price of coca to less than 20 bolivianos a load and the subsequent drop in arrests and seizures performed by the UMOPAR.[17] The threat of NAU officials to penalize the UMOPAR for what they viewed as a poor performance shows the way in which the goal of paralyzing drug traffic through efficiency is overridden by bureaucratic concern about reports to Washington enumerating arrests and seizures. Bureaucratic paradoxes of this sort often arise as a consequence of attaching predominant value to forms and procedures instead of matters of substance.[18]

The value attached to procedures and forms[19] has been illustrated throughout this book, and a 1990 case regarding seven jeeps is another example of the predominant importance of procedure. As a consequence of a shortage of vehicles that could operate in the jungle, the NAU headquarters in La Paz lent seven jeeps to the DEA in Chimoré. When NAU personnel in the Chapare discovered that the jeeps had been utilized by the Bolivian UMOPAR, the NAU in La Paz immediately took the jeeps away, overlooking statements that they had been used on urgent enforcement missions. The jeeps were returned to the Chimoré compound only when the head of the U.S. special forces in the Chapare, Captain Adam Sanchez, complained vociferously about what he considered a ridiculous decision.[20]

The desire to make agency records look good by destroying stomping pits explains an otherwise baffling lack of reaction toward large cocaine transactions[21] and also explains the Huanchaca fiasco. Abundant evidence about the large laboratories processing hydrochloride in Huanchaca did not result in any action on the part of U.S. or Bolivian enforcers. As a consequence of the enforcers' imperviousness, three innocent civilians were assassinated, no arrests were made on the spot, and large hydrochloride laboratories that could have been destroyed were dismantled by their operators who comfortably left the site, presumably with a large amount of cocaine hydrochloride, only to reemerge on the same spot in 1990.[22] Raiding large laboratories is time consuming and dangerous; it is also futile if dossiers may be improved simply by burning stomping pits or by destroying small paste kitchens.[23]

A similar example of such a distorted practice is the case of Vueltadero,[24] in which regular coca paste pickups had been reported to the DEA and the UMOPAR, but no arrests were made until civilian Bolivian officials took matters into their own hands.[25] Two reasons were given to explain the failure of the enforcers to act: The commander of the Bolivian UMOPAR had a direct connection with the traffickers who were responsible for the pickups, and the DEA would not trust any data stemming from sources other than its own informants.[26]

The previous examples deal with the U.S. bureaucratic proneness to produce gross contradictions between the pursued goals of enforcement and the way enforcement is actually carried out. There is a parallel between these visible incongruities and the logic of the Bolivian agencies' behavior at the same bureaucratic level. Since the country's return to democratic rule in 1982, the United States has started looking at Bolivia as meriting more political attention and financial aid. The UMOPAR corps is trained and equipped by the United States,[27] and the Bolivian armed forces are also endowed with U.S. gear, which will be considerably increased once the army fully engages in the war.[28] The importance of the Bolivian coca/cocaine trade for the United States has placed Bolivia on the world's political map—as is also illustrated by the presence of Italian, French, and UN technicians in the Chapare.

Drugs have a great importance for the Bolivian economy and politics, and for bureaus involved in drug enforcement, the current state of affairs is ideal in a special way. Under present circumstances, only the drug trade can give Bolivia an international importance, and if the cocaine industry is finally curbed, there will be no reason for the United States to help maintain the UMOPAR or to allot resources to army and naval units. It is also true, however, that the failure of these agencies to produce positive results means, in the long run, curtailment of U.S. aid. The optimal situation consists, therefore, of an everlasting battle to encourage the First World to invest in a seemingly promising antidrug campaign.

Drug enforcement is in Bolivia to stay, and there are "natural correctives" that ensure that success in the war on drugs will be moderate at the most. These correctives are, first, a generalized "compenetration" of bureaucrats and traffickers; second, competition among agencies; and third, "clientelism."

3. THE SINGULARITY OF BOLIVIA'S "CORRUPTION"

In Bolivia, the lack of a common perception of historical events is a bar to the attainment of consensus on coca and cocaine policies, and the absence of a set of acknowledged normative parameters to assess events frustrates the existence of a standard version of the country's institutional, political, and economic realities. In applying different references, contemporary interest sectors—including each of the armed forces and the police—support contradictory versions of Bolivia's situation with respect to coca and cocaine. Indeed, as is illustrated in Chapters 2 and 4, discourse about the country's coca/cocaine policy is often a vehicle for the negotiation of sectorial interests—both connected with the cocaine issue and in other areas.

In this setting, the war image is not only inappropriate but inevitably bound for failure, as "war" implies a win/lose proposition, not a trade-off of interests. There are at least two reasons deriving from the complexity of the interests involved that make the war on drugs in Bolivia implausible. First, the lack of sufficiently coercive state institutions has made the illegal sector, and the coca/cocaine sector in particular, too large to be excluded from joint, concerted policies. Second, the plethora of actively conflictive interest groups render a war at less than an unbearable cost impossible, and even consensus is infeasible without some compromise. The Huanchaca case and the ensuing judicial behavior described in Chapter 3 illustrate the latter point.

This situation means that the value-laden concept of *corruption* is misleading when applied to Bolivian officials. The notion of corruption, the First World's conception of it in particular, derives its value force from the idea of an actor undercutting a set of rules that society lives by to attain a personal or sectorial position of influence, wealth, or power.[29] The term is usually attached to the existence of institutions that the majority of the populace acknowledge as legitimate, that is, to the existence of formal legality. The sizable presence of drug interests in Bolivia's official sectors reveals the extreme weakness of the country's economy and political institutions, their want of universal legitimacy, and, in consequence, their limited authority.[30] Instead, corporatism and clientelism have dominated Bolivia's political economy through a web of social ties that vertically link members from all social classes into anomic sectors and segments largely on the basis of personalism.[31]

The usual notion of corruption blurs an understanding of the dynamics by which changing groups interact: Today, it is a commonly accepted practice in many countries for officials to levy "taxes" to allow illicit activities to continue.[32] Thus, the dynamics of interest groups as they relate to the coca/cocaine issue can only be accurately understood in context, and the idea of "compenetration" provides a clearer picture of the situation in Bolivia than the one of corruption does.

"Compenetration" means not only being bought off by cocaine money but also accepting a varied range of blessings from cocaine businesspeople,[33] including employment. High UMOPAR officers complain that after receiving specialized training in survival and jungle warfare at the Garras del Valor course in Chimoré, Leopardo personnel align themselves with traffickers who are ready to pay them well.[34] Thus, drug enforcement is plagued by antagonistic interests from within the state apparatus. Such interests, for example, underlie the reported misuse of U.S. aid by the Bolivian armed forces.[35] According to one complaint, the navy's Piranha boats, a contribution from the United States, have been used to ferry drug-processing materials and cocaine.

4. BOLIVIA'S INTERAGENCY FRICTION

The second "natural" corrective that ensures unsuccessful enforcement is the existing friction between Bolivian enforcement agencies. The Santa Ana de Yacuma case reflects the extreme antagonism underlying armed struggles between the UMOPAR and naval personnel,[36] and the army and the UMOPAR display their conflicting interests through scuffles such as those described in Chapter 4.[37] There are historical grounds for the existing interagency grudges that hamper enforcement, but the primary reason seems to lie in the race unleashed among them all to obtain the largest possible slice of foreign resources. The behavior of the Bolivian agencies is a clear example of sectorial interests overriding national policy.

Thus, compenetration and intrastate frictions result in flagrant policy paradoxes. A salient aspect of the interagency competition is that adding resources by engaging additional agencies overwhelms drug control instead of facilitating it, as was demonstrated by President Siles-Suazo's order to have the army control the Chapare in 1984.[38] Internal conflict displaces the overall goal, which makes the chances of success illusory. A high U.S. military officer who participated in Operation Blast Furnace[39] declared after the fiasco that the agencies' coordination was unmanageable.

5. "CLIENTELISM"

Besides compenetration and internal competition, political "clientelism" in Bolivia also helps hinder effective enforcement campaigns.[40] In 1990, when news circulated in Bolivia that Carlos Arauz had been removed from the Dirección de la Coca Legal after President Paz-Zamora's inauguration, the price of coca suddenly boosted from 60 bolivianos to over 110 bolivianos a load, showing that business had suddenly become more promising.[41] Knowing the reputation Arauz enjoyed for his efficiency, replacing him was seen as the cause of the sharp increase in the price of raw coca.[42] Had efficiency been highly regarded in Bolivia, Arauz's position should have been granted permanence to remove it from the vagaries of everyday politics. The standing practice, however, is that new administrations dispose of as many posts as possible, including those for which experience is crucial. As in most South American countries and many others, political favors are rewarded with appointments to public office, a practice that can have negative effects. Hugo Cochamanidis, the Paz-Zamora administration's head of Dirección de la Coca Legal, candidly confessed to me that his lack of experience has made it difficult for him to fill Arauz's shoes.[43]

6. HOW U.S. AND BOLIVIAN BUREAUCRACIES INTERACT

To maintain that there is "connivance" between U.S. and Bolivian bureaucracies or an explicit "understanding" between both countries' antidrug agencies that leads to shortcomings and common flaws is to overstate the situation. However, there are persistent ways in which the concerns of the U.S. and Bolivian bureaucracies interact. This book provides several examples that show not only the way in which those interests contravene their countries' general interest but also the way in which the overgrown enforcement agencies of both countries tend to adapt to each other's methods through their parallel errors. Their shortcomings lead to shared irregularities, misguided tactics, and common omissions.

A prime example of such shared irregularities is offered in Chapter 1 where I describe a situation that occurred in Chimoré in 1987–1988.[44] The Camba lawyer Emma Zalarza, known to be closely connected to the cocaine industry, moved into the Chimoré outpost with her lover, Colonel Nicolas Anaya, at that time the UMOPAR unit's top officer. Despite Zalarza's reputation, she and Anaya often shared a table at the officers' club with personnel of the special forces and the DEA.[45] On those occasions, the U.S. and Bolivian enforcers openly discussed their activities, thus supplying Zalarza with valuable intelligence data. There are other similar cases of this kind of negligence.

After a January 1990 visit to Chimoré, U.S. Congressman John Conyers's group described the compound as having been turned into a brothel where prostitutes freely walked in and out. Their account also charged U.S. personnel, and DEA agents in particular, of at least condoning such goings-on by omitting to report them.[46] Such behavior seriously affects enforcers' discipline and consequently imperils their efficiency. Furthermore, the account deserves special consideration because Chapare prostitutes are known to often be traffickers' informants.[47]

The adaptation of Bolivian and U.S. bureaucracies in Bolivia is illustrated by many examples in this book, but three important events in particular clarify the point: first, the trend to concentrate enforcement efforts on coca stompers while neglecting major traffickers, despite the contradictory consequences of this policy;[48] second, the perplexities posed by the irregular handling of the Huanchaca and Vueltadero episodes, in which action against greater misdeeds was flagrantly overlooked;[49] and third, the gross inaccuracies in reporting coca eradication.[50] There are many more examples throughout the previous chapters portraying the accommodation of U.S. and Bolivian enforcers, but those three events are clear enough to illustrate the point. The first two are narrowly interconnected and provide a picture of a U.S.-Bolivian joint approach to enforcement. The third issue shows the way deliberate inaccuracies accumulated in both Bolivian and U.S. agencies.

Some Chapareños and outside observers have charged that DEA personnel, together with the UMOPAR[51] have actively participated in criminal activities against the peasants in the Beni region. Following complaints from the Catholic church and human rights organizations, a Bolivian Senate commission was established to investigate these alleged transgressions which consisted of physical abuse and misappropriation of money and goods.[52] Representing the commission, Senator Jorge Barrientos declared that neither the UMOPAR nor the DEA had answered to thirty-two specific indictments of serious abuses.[53] However accurate the complaints against the DEA's participation, it cannot be denied that U.S. officers in Bolivia work closely with the UMOPAR agents and are well acquainted with their daily activities. In the best possible case, the DEA must have at least consented to the transgressions.

The eradication effort also shows how U.S. and Bolivian bureaucracies work together to promote their sectorial interests through deliberate inaccuracies, and technical departments dealing with coca/cocaine elimination are also illustrative examples of such interagency cooperation. Warnings about the oddities of the eradication effort did not deter Bolivian and U.S. officials from submitting the results to their bosses who allegedly elected to look the other way.[54] The maneuver enabled Bolivia to obtain funds from the United States on the basis of deceitful figures.

7. THE WEIGHT OF OFFICIALS' PERSONAL INTERESTS

On a "personal bureaucratic" level, personal reasons lead officials to attempt to optimize their own situations.[55] Performance records and political achievements are thus targeted by bureaucrats as being of prime importance at the expense of the two countries' general interest. For instance, U.S. personnel seem to pursue promotions by averting risks as much as possible. It is sometimes difficult to distinguish between disruptive sectorial action and individual self-regarding activity, but it is obvious that improving the reputation of Bolivian and U.S. agencies operating in Bolivia has a direct bearing on the reputation of the heads of those agencies. The entire debate about bringing in the Bolivian Army is impregnated with both sectorial and personal motivations, as is shown by the reasons enunciated for either justifying or opposing such intervention.

The Ministry of Justice and the Interior, with jurisdiction over the UMOPAR, vehemently declared that it was more than unlikely that traffickers ever exceeded the force's capacities. Simultaneously, representatives of the Ministry of Defense said the army needed to be called in because the UMOPAR had already been overwhelmed. These views expose the bureaucratic paradox the Paz-Zamora administration was confronted with. On the one hand, it had to demonstrate that its zeal in the war on drugs was eliciting sound achievements. On the other hand, Bolivia had to meet its commitment to the United States to involve the army in the war on drugs. The solution, according to the interpretation of law 1008, involved acknowledging that the police forces had been overwhelmed.[56] In the controversy, high officials tried to prove that their respective departments were essential to the anticocaine campaign, and their opinions were anything but objective assessments of Bolivia's reality. Rather, they expressed the interests of the officials from different areas in their struggle to obtain the largest political and financial dividends from either engaging or not engaging the army in the war on drugs.

The way personal interests affect national policies is evident throughout this book, but a prime example of the way self-centered interests override the general interest is DEA agents' standing practice of withholding information from the rest of the agency's personnel, including close comrades. Bolivian officers of the State Department affirm that DEA officers refuse to share information gathered from personal sources,[57] the logic being that agents are reluctant to share the merits of their own individual accomplishments with other colleagues. If success is confined to only one agent, that person accrues maximum credit, which might lead to a promotion. The practice is also applied on a larger scale. When each one of the DEA teams based in the Chapare is replaced every two or three months,[58] it leaves no data for the new group. Hence, each team is forced to start from scratch. Only personal aspirations can explain this apparently senseless behavior.[59]

The logic of self-promotion appears to provide grounds for the "internationalization" of the jungle warfare course Garras del Valor.[60] The futility of inviting European agents to join a course that specializes in jungle survival and warfare has no explanation but personal promotion of the U.S. Embassy officials and Bolivian authorities who cosponsored the invitations. This expansion of the course participants involved a useless investment to train agents who had never seen or had ever imagined they would visit a jungle in their entire lives. This use of the course for public relations was also carried out at the expense of shrinking its capability to instruct Bolivian officers, for whom the training is crucial.

8. TO CONCLUDE

The Bolivian war on drugs is fraught with paradoxes. Perhaps the greatest of all of these paradoxes is the new social environment that U.S. policy has helped create, and in that environment, coca cultivation and drug manufacturing are ceaselessly expanding. As long as cocaine continues to be a cherished commodity in the First World, nothing indicates that the present situation will change as a consequence of current policies, and if that condition does change Bolivia will not improve its present economic or institutional plight.

If new production sources or synthetic chemicals replace Bolivian cocaine in the streets of New York, Chicago, Rome, and Frankfurt, Bolivia will suffer the consequences of the "war" bureaucracies, and it is likely that the developed world will have to invest once again in Bolivia to help the government face the nightmare of a new Peruvian-like Shining Path or Tupac Amaru, Argentinean Montoneros, or Colombian M19. The current campaign has not only failed to improve the country's economy but has also led to an increased weakening of its institutions.

A love/hate relationship between governance and bureaucracy is seen by political scientists as an inevitable fact of life. In the case of the war on drugs in Bolivia, overgrown bureaucratic agencies offer a clear demonstration of the existence of a structurally perverse system. Although this book does not offer a clear solution to the flow of cocaine from Bolivia into the United States, the conclusion it reaches may be considered as a step toward a correct answer: Bolivia and the United States must terminate the perverse war on drugs approach. The current policy may well lead to carrying out the suggestion once made by a U.S. Embassy official in La Paz that the only way to sort out U.S. problems in the region is to "abolish Bolivia."[61]

NOTES

1. James M. Malloy, "Authoritarianism and Corporatism: The Case of Bolivia," in *Authoritarianism and Corporatism in Latin America*, ed. James M. Malloy, (Pittsburgh: University of Pittsburgh Press, 1979), p. 459.

2. Jorge Alderete, under-secretary of social defense in the Paz-Estenssoro administration, espoused this view vehemently in an interview in La Paz, September 12, 1989. Eudoro Barrientos, head of a *cocalero* union in Villanueva, was also of this opinion (interview, May 29, 1990), as were a number of Chapareños I met, such as Victor, a former cocaine transporter and ex–trade union leader in San Francisco port (interview in San Francisco, Bolivia, January 16, 1990). See also Michael Painter, *Institutional Analysis of the Chapare Regional Development*

Project (CRDP) (Institute for Development Anthropology, Clark University, Worcester, Massachusetts, and Institute for Development Anthropology, Binghamton, New York, 1990), p. 42.

3. Whatever the outcome in Bolivia, it is also true that, according to some authors, U.S. officials, some of whom serve in the State Department, consider the overall conception of the war on drugs a consequence of political rhetoric and have little hope that the strategy will work (see Ethan A. Nadelman, "Cops Across Borders: Transnational Crime and International Law Enforcement" [Ph.D. dissertation, Harvard University, Department of Government, June 1987], p. 260).

4. Even at the State Department there is lack of concern for the drug issue at the highest levels, and as a consequence, the renegotiation of contracts that could have helped the Andean countries out of their economic plight while diversifying their economies was simply neglected.

5. See U.S. Congress, Committee on Government Operations, "Thirty-Eighth Report: United States Anti-Narcotics Activities in the Andean Region" (Washington, D.C., August 30, 1990), p. 10.

6. A U.S. diplomat in La Paz expressed this view to me on May 23, 1990.

7. The capacity of trade organizations to react strongly to the imperilment of the coca/cocaine trade has been demonstrated by the mobilization of thousands of *cocaleros* and their supporters to obstruct communication among different vital centers in the country. Coca growers have become the country's unions' strongest clientele (see, for example, Kevin Healy, "Coca, the State, and Peasantry in Bolivia, 1982–1988," *Journal of Interamerican Studies and World Affairs* 30:2–3 [Summer/Fall 1988], pp. 105–126).

8. The distinction is also between "logical" and "pragmatic" paradoxes. By logical paradoxes, I refer to propositions that are inherently contradictory; for instance, "Ignore this remark! Be free!" It is simply impossible to ignore a signal that constitutes a reason to do or not to do something, and the command to be free cannot be followed without negating its own existence. "Pragmatic" paradoxes are those in which the contradictions appear once the texts acquire a certain meaning through interpretation. For instance, there is nothing paradoxical about the proposition, "Efficient enforcement of drug laws—that is, performing arrests and seizures—lowers the price of coca leaf and thereby encourages cultivators to find a new source of income." The paradox emerges (as described in Chapter 4) once the procedure is construed as attaching independent value to the arrests and seizures as ends in themselves. If arrests and seizures succeed in bringing down the price of coca, coca/cocaine transactions necessarily diminish, but a drop in the cocaine business brings about a parallel plunge in the number of arrests and seizures, which are valued as goals. Whatever the outcome, such an interpretation of the proposition ensures frustration.

9. See Chapter 1, sections 4 and 5.

10. Oscar Oszlak and Guillermo O'Donnell, *Estado y politicas estatales en America Latina: Hacia una estrategia de investigacion*, CEDES document/G.E. CLACSO, no. 4 (Buenos Aires, 1976).

11. For President Reagan's secret directive issued in 1986, see Nadelman, "Cops Across Borders," p. 225.

12. There is hardly a Latin American country that the United States does not consider responsible for failing to control the drug business. In Bolivia and Peru, 80–90 percent of the world's circulating coca is grown, and cocaine is semirefined and fully refined. Coca is also grown in Ecuador and Colombia, and marijuana grows in Colombia and Paraguay. Trafficking organizations operate from Colombia and Brazil, and Argentina, Chile, Uruguay, Brazil, the Bahamas, Honduras, and Guatemala are considered transit or transhipment countries. Belize, Panama, the Cayman Islands, and Uruguay are money laundering havens. Panama enjoys a special status because of Noriega's alleged personal involvement in sundry drug related activities, and Nicaragua and Cuba have been accused of cooperating with drug traffickers for economic and/or political reasons. Thus, it is hard to remove one single Central or South American nation from the U.S. antidrug quest.

13. See Chapter 2, section 2.

14. Interviews with a NAU agent in La Paz, May 26, 1990, and an UMOPAR officer in Chimoré, May 28, 1990.

15. For a study of bureaucracies' behavior, see Oscar Oszlak, "Notas criticas para una teoria de la burocracia estatal," in *Teoria de la burocracia estatal*, ed. Oscar Oszlak (Buenos Aires, Argentina: Paidos, 1984), p. 284.

16. The inclination I refer to is revealed by an ex–DEA veteran, Michael Levine: I, "too, believed that DEA was corrupt, but in a totally different way. Wheeler believed the whole agency was taking graft and selling drugs. I believed the suits [in DEA jargon, "suits" are bureaucrats who are not involved in undercover or risky tasks] were lying to the American public to perpetuate the funding of the agency and its programs and, of course, their jobs; not to mention parlaying their easy access to the media into more lucrative careers in the private sector and politics; along with a host of other reasons that had nothing to do with winning the drug war" (Michael Levine, *Deep Cover: The Inside Story of How DEA Infighting and Subterfuge Lost Us the Biggest Battle of the Drug War* [New York: Delacorte Press, 1990], p. 159). My view, however, is more encompassing because my research shows that deceit is a structural feature of the agency at most levels of decisionmaking and implementation. I admit I have gathered no data concerning undercover agents.

17. See Chapter 4, section 3.

18. For a distinction between "procedural" and "substantive" bureaucratic responsiveness and the intertwining of ends and means, see Douglas T. Yates, Jr., "Hard Choices: Justifying Bureaucratic Decisions," in *Public Duties: The Moral Obligation of Government Officials*, ed. Joel L. Fleischman et al. (Cambridge, Mass. and London: Harvard University Press, 1981), p. 32.

19. One may also apply Lars Schoultz's terminology when he refers to the pursuance of "sub-goals" or "means" as goals in themselves (Lars Schoultz, *National Security and United States Policy Toward Latin America* [Princeton: Princeton University Press, 1987], p. 35).

20. Interview with two high-ranking officers in Chimoré, May 29, 1990.

21. An example of the opposite stance equally illustrates the point. The following is a disclosure by a high official of the Argentine Gendarmerie in August 1988 in Buenos Aires when I was the solicitor to the Supreme Court: "Relations

with the U.S. [DEA] have always been peculiar. We never ever got from the DEA the information we expected, and we knew they had it. On its tour, the DEA undertook the most extravagant ventures. Very few basic paste stomping pits were found in Argentina territory over the 1970s and 1980s. We have never heard of cocaine laboratories in this country except for a few located in the jungle on the border with Bolivia. Despite this fact, operation Nomo was envisaged by a regional DEA official by the name of Phillips. This idea followed the U.S. State Department's accusation that the Argentinean enforcement agencies were not doing their job. A search operation, Nomo, was addressed at detecting and destroying laboratories in Argentina's northwest. As I said, we never heard of such laboratories existing in this country, and the DEA never supplied any data as to the reality of the target. It is no surprise that laboratories were never even detected, and as a result, the Argentinean branch of the DEA was placed under receivership. The head, an ex-cop from Baltimore, was reassigned. He was replaced by a Texan who made everybody feel he was above them. He did not do any better. One thing was clear: the National Gendarmerie's unequivocal objection to bringing cocaine into Argentina for whatever purpose, as the DEA wanted. This was perceived of by the DEA officers in Buenos Aires as a sheer demonstration of enmity." (The Argentine Gendarmerie is a militarized corps that guards Argentina's borders.)

22. Although gossip about the rebirth of drug-related activities in Huanchaca has spread among Chapare enforcers, a major of the UMOPAR that I met in Ivirgarzama, Chapare, claimed to have detailed information about this issue. Also, Cochabamba television journalist Elva Morales (interview in a bar in the town of Cochabamba on January 15, 1990).

23. "The result of the misplaced emphasis on microlevel indicators of success may be inaccurate and/or misleading information provided to Congress. 'Overly positive' International Narcotics Control Strategy Reports (INCSRs) are one example" (U.S. Congress, Committee on Government Operations, "Thirty-Eighth Report"), p. 31.

24. See Chapter 2, section 4.

25. See Ibid.

26. Gustavo Araujo, an UMOPAR officer and a NAU official, gave this explanation to me on October 2, 1990, when I visited the village of Vueltadero, Chapare. Another UMOPAR official who was present at the interview agreed with Gustavo's version.

27. See Chapter 2, section 1.

28. See Chapter 4, section 4.

29. Michael Johnston, "Corruption Inequality and Change," in *Corruption, Development, and Inequality*, ed. Peter M. Ward (London and New York: Routledge, 1989), p. 15.

30. Bolivia has never enjoyed the benefits of a strong formal institutional system. Anthony Henman writes: "The impunity with which the leading traffickers operate in Bolivia raises the question of the limits of state authority in the context of a diffuse narcocracy. Not a single government—whether of the left, right or center, established by force or elected by popular vote—has been without scandal and well documented cases of corruption, most often in the very organs supposedly

constituted to repress the illicit drug trade. Indeed, corruption may well be a misnomer in such a situation, and one should think instead in terms of *compenetration*. In this view, positions of official authority are the object of political contest in order to define who has the right to levy unofficial taxes on the cocaine business. A posting to one of the narcotics police forces—where salaries hover characteristically around 50 dollars a month—would thus still constitute a plum opportunity for the economic advancement of middle-echelon bureaucrats. The same would be true, for the younger officers, of a military command in the Chapare, the Beni or Santa Cruz" (Henman, "Cocaine Futures," in *The Big Deal: The Politics of the Illicit Drugs Business*, ed. Anthony Henman, Roger Lewis, and Tim Malyon [London and Sydney: Pluto Press, 1985], p. 155).

31. Much has been written about the sectorial and anomic structure of Bolivian society, including Malloy, "Authoritarianism and Corporatism"; Jonathan Kelley and Herbert Klein, *Revolution and the Rebirth of Inequality* (Berkeley: University of California Press, 1981); and James Dunkerley, *Rebellion in the Veins: Political Struggle in Bolivia 1952–1982* (London: Verso, 1984).

32. Henman, "Cocaine Futures," p. 155.

33. See Chapter 3 and the aftermath of the Huanchaca incident. Among the multiplicity of such episodes, Bolivian newspapers in La Paz reported in December 1989 that four important traffickers had escaped from different detention centers, including the outpost of Chimoré, which is the headquarters of the DEA, U.S. special forces, and the UMOPAR. The police continually fail to comply with their obligation to place detainees under the jurisdiction of the courts. Instead, the UMOPAR and narcotics divisions hold detainees in different police compounds in Santa Cruz and the Chapare. Sources quoted by the La Paz newspapers indicate that stories that the escapees have to climb the compound's fence in order to escape are a distortion of the facts. According to one source, one detainee walked out without custodians boasting a written authorization (see Hugo Quintana Jaldin, "Incumplimiento de leyes ocasionó la fuga de 4 narcotraficantes en menos de 24 dias," *Ultima Hora*, May 22, 1990; see also *Presencia*, December 3 and 6, 1989).

34. One of the heads of the Garras del Valor course asserts that defections of officers hired by traffickers after basic training are not uncommon (interview in the Chapare, May 29, 1990).

35. See the version of the report of the U.S. Congress Subcommittee on Information, Justice and Agriculture, published in *Ultima Hora*, August 30, 1990.

36. See Chapter 2, section 8.

37. See Chapter 4, section 3.

38. See Chapter 2, section 1.

39. See Chapter 2, section 2.

40. See Malloy, "Authoritarianism and Corporatism," p. 459, and Colin Sage, "Drugs and Economic Development in Latin America: A Study in the Political Bolivian Economy of Cocaine in Bolivia," in *Corruption, Development, and Inequality*, ed. Peter M. Ward (London and New York: Routledge, 1989), p. 44.

41. Although Paz-Zamora stepped in in August 1989, Carlos Arauz was not replaced until January 1990. Only personal prestige may have kept Arauz in his

post given that in Bolivia, shifts in the national bureaucracies occur almost immediately after a new administration is inaugurated.

42. Interview with Enrique Valverde, Villa Tunari, September 15, 1989.

43. Interview in La Paz main office of the Dirección de la Coca Legal on September 28, 1990.

44. See Chapter 1, section 5.

45. Interviews with two different NAU officials in the Chapare; one on May 28, 1990, and the other on October 2, 1990.

46. The Bolivian media reported alleged statements by members of the commission who accompanied Congressman Conyers, member of the Subcommittee on Information, Justice, and Agriculture (see *Ultima Hora*, August 30, 1990). Manuel Benitez-Larroca claims that the DEA would not participate in shoot-outs against drug traffickers because of the possibility of major conflicts if peasants suffered casualties; however, Benitez explains, DEA agents had no qualms about leading the UMOPAR when it broke into the homes of campesinos (Manuel Benitez-Larroca, "UMOPAR libra una batalla desigual contra el narcotráfico en Chapare," *Presencia*, March 18, 1990).

47. On September 16, 1989, the head of NAU in Cochabamba at that time, Enrique Valverde, drove me to Puerto Villarroel in the Chapare. Being repeatedly accosted by prostitutes who posed ceaseless questions, Valverde explained that many of them in that area were either permanently employed or paid for each piece of information by the Camba traffickers. The head of the Garras del Valor course in Chimoré, Captain Mario Ayala, supplied the same information in an interview held on May 29, 1990.

48. See Chapter 2, sections 2 and 4.

49. See Chapter 2, section 4, and Chapter 3, section 1.

50. See Chapter 4, section 2.

51. Elva Morales has specialized in following these events in the Chapare region, and I interviewed her in the city of Cochabamba on January 15, 1990. I also interviewed two *cocaleros* from Villanueva, Pablo and Julio, whom NAU officials knew, on September 16, 1989.

52. Denunciations from the pastoral secretariat of the Catholic church and serious concern on the part of human rights activists are reflected in the Senate investigation reported in *Presencia*, April 4, 1990.

53. Ibid.

54. See Chapter 4, section 2.

55. For a study of the distinction between self- and public interest, see Joel L. Fleishman, "Self-Interest and Political Integrity," in *Public Duties: The Moral Obligation of Government Officials*, ed. Joel L. Fleishman et al., (Cambridge, Mass. and London: Harvard University Press, 1981), p. 52.

56. See Chapter 4, section 4.

57. Statements obtained in interviews with a NAU employee in Chimoré, May 28, 1990, and an UMOPAR officer on May 29, 1990, coincided.

58. Statements of the chief of the special forces, General Añez, published in *Ultima Hora*, April 19, 1990. The U.S. Committee on Government Operations went further and said, "many of the DEA were on ninety-day temporary assign-

ment from the United States and could not speak Spanish" (U.S. Congress, Committee on Government Operations, "Thirty-Eighth Report"), p. 25.

59. Lack of communication is especially obvious at the level of interagency cooperation: "Part of the [lack of communication] problem can be traced to legitimate differences in their respective institutional missions, attitudes, and the operational approaches, according to the Senate investigation, which seem to prompt almost inherent conflicts between and among them" (U.S. Congress, Committee on Government Operations, "Thirty-Eighth Report"), p. 23.

60. See Chapter 4, section 4.

61. See Schoultz, *National Security and United States Policy toward Latin America*, p. 34.

Postscript

At one point, an interesting discussion took place at a seminar on drug policy held at the School of International Affairs, Columbia University. Although the scholars participating in the debate largely endorsed the view that decriminalization of drug offenses is a necessary step, the reasons behind that view varied considerably. The main arguments were based on the threat to civil liberties that enforcing drug laws poses; the costs of enforcement; the morality of meddling in other people's privacy; the deterioration of international relations as a consequence of U.S. efforts to crack down on drug production and traffic; and the inability of the current attempts to cope with the drug trade.

This book draws upon the last argument in a roundabout way. My main point is that drug offenses erase any possible borders between two different types of countries: strong states and states that are unable to impose rules of social control upon their populations.[1] Drug enforcement has demonstrated the relativity of this categorization: The relative strengths of the nations do not matter in the war on drugs. The strength or weakness of states must be assessed by the segment of the population they aim to control through specific coercive policies. Criminalizing vast sectors of a population necessarily weakens the authority of the state, especially when coercion is addressed to averting "victimless crime."

This simple truth has been acknowledged in the United States. The growth of enforcement agencies as a consequence of Prohibition and the criminalization of the drug trade and consumption has provoked countless discussions in political and academic circles. Some people have focused on the immorality of enforcing morality, others have stressed the danger that legislation such as the Harrison and Volstead Acts of 1914 and 1919, and the ensuing enlargening of police bureaucracies to enforce those laws, attempt to control our personal lives.[2] Drug enforcement today seems to illustrate in a most dramatic way the futility of enforcing morality. In this book, I have described a war that is not only extremely costly to both Bolivia and the United States but also counterproductive on almost all counts.

In September 1990, when the first draft of the manuscript for this book was finished, I realized that my research had carried me far beyond the theses I was ready to espouse when my work on Bolivia commenced. In the beginning, my aim was confined to pointing out the way a contradiction-ridden campaign was being waged, but I could not help concluding that drug enforcement traps governments in an inescapable quandary. Antidrug coercion advocates must come to terms with an inevitable alternative. They must either deal with drug production and traffic with insufficient human resources or enlarge enforcement agencies in such a way that these bureaucracies will escape government control. Although it is true that bureaucratic agencies develop their own interests, which conflict with what political theorists call the "general interest," size adds an extra element. When these departments grow beyond a certain size, the central state apparatus loses its capability to subordinate them to the interests it embodies. Thus, experience shows that in Bolivia, the DEA/NAU complex has developed its own strategies in the pursuance of its sectorial convenience. The U.S. Justice and State Departments, which supposedly oversee these agencies, have no way to further the U.S. perceived general interest; the monster has grown too big to be kept under control.

The conclusion seems as strong as it is ineluctable. Repressing drug offenses becomes an impossible endeavor because agencies to deal with the effort are either too small or too big. Regular-police forces are not designed to control the sizable number of drug law transgressors as the number of lawbreakers has increased perhaps two- or threefold. However, if enforcement agencies are enlarged to meet the imposing number of drug offenders, they become too large to remain loyal to their targeted goals as defined by the top political officials.

NOTES

1. An interesting discussion of this topic is presented in Joel S. Migdal, *Strong Societies and Weak States: State Societies Relations and State Capabilities in the Third World* (Princeton: Princeton University Press, 1988).

2. See, for example, Evelyn Parks, "From Constabulary to Police Society: Implications for Social Control," in *The Criminologist: Crime and the Criminal*, ed. Charles E. Reasons (Pacific Palisades, Calif.: Goodyear Publishing Company, 1974), p. 271. The Volstead Act was antialcohol; the Harrison Act was antidrugs.

Selected Bibliography

Aguilar-Gomez, Anibal. "El impacto desestructurador del capital paralelo sobre la economia campesina," *Procampo* (La Paz), November 1987.

Albó, Xavier, and Liberman, Kitula, et al. *Para comprender las culturas rurales en Bolivia*. La Paz: Ministerio de Educacion y Cultura, 1989.

Andreas, Peter, and Youngers, Coletta. "U.S. Drug Policy and the Andean Cocaine Industry." *World Policy Journal* 6 (1989), pp. 529–562.

Bedregal-Gutierrez, Guillermo, and Vizcarra-Pando, Ruddy. *La lucha boliviana contra la agresión del narcotrafico*. La Paz: Los Amigos del Libro, 1989.

Benitez-Larroca, Manuel. "UMOPAR libra una batalla desigual contra el narcotráfico en Chapare." *Presencia* (La Paz), March 18, 1990.

Blanes, Jose, and Calderón, Fernando, et al. *Tras nuevas raices: Migraciones internas y colonizacion en Bolivia*. La Paz: Proyecto Politico de Poblacion, Ministerio de Planeamiento, n.d.

Campodónico, Humberto. "La política del aveztruz." In *Coca, cocaina, y narcotráfico: Laberinto en los Andes*, ed. Diego García-Sayán. Lima: Comisión Andina de Juristas, 1989.

Castro, Juan Jose, and Gomez, Walter. "Crisis economica y perspectivas de la democracia." In *Democracía a la deriva: Dilemas de la participación y concertación social en Bolivia*. La Paz: PNUD, CLACSO, CERES, 1987.

Crandon, Libbet. *From the Fat of Our Souls*. Berkeley and Los Angeles: University of California Press, 1990.

Delaine, Bernard Louis. *Coca Farming in the Chapare: A Form of Collective Innovation*. Ph.D. dissertation, Saint Louis University. Ann Arbor, Mich.: University Microfilms International, 1990.

Doria-Medina, Samuel. *La economia informal en Bolivia*. La Paz: Editorial Offset Boliviana Limitada, 1986.

Dunkerley, James. *Rebellion in the Veins: Political Struggle in Bolivia 1952–1982*. London: Verso, 1984.

Eckstein, Susan. "Transformation of a 'Revolution from Below': Bolivia and International Capitalism." *Comparative Studies in Society and History* 25 (1983), p. 205.

Fleishman, Joel L. "Self-Interest and Political Integrity." In *Public Duties: The Moral Obligation of Government Officials*, ed. Joel L. Fleishman et al. Cambridge, Mass. and London: Harvard University Press, 1981.

Flores, Gonzalo, and Blanes, José. *Donde va el Chapare?* Cochabamba, Bolivia: Centro de Estudios de la Realidad Economica y Social, 1984.

Gamba-Stonehouse, Virginia. "Missions and Strategy: The Argentine Example." In *The Military and Democracy: The Future of Civil-Military Relations in Latin America*, ed. Louis Goodman et al. Lexington, Mass. and Toronto: Lexington Books, 1990.

Goodman, Louis, and Mendelson, Johanna S. R. "The Threat of New Missions: Latin American Militaries and the Drug War." In *The Military and Democracy: The Future of Civil-Military Relations in Latin America*, ed. Louis Goodman et al. Lexington, Mass. and Toronto: Lexington Books, 1990.

Healy, Kevin. "The Boom Within the Crisis: Some Recent Effects of Foreign Cocaine Markets on Bolivian Rural Society and Economy." In *Coca and Cocaine: Effects on People and Policy in Latin America*, ed. Deborah Paccini and Christine Franquemont. Cultural Survival Report, Latin American Studies Program. Ithaca, N.Y.: Cornell University, 1985.

──────. "Coca, the State, and Peasantry in Bolivia, 1982–1988." *Journal of Interamerican Studies and World Affairs* 30:2–3 (Summer/Fall 1988), pp. 105–126.

Henman, Anthony. "Cocaine Futures." In *Big Deal: The Politics of the Illicit Drugs Business*, ed. Anthony Henman, Roger Lewis, and Tim Malyon. London and Sydney: Pluto Press, 1985.

Inciardi, James A. *The War on Drugs: Heroin, Cocaine, Crime, and Public Policy*. Mountain View, Calif.: Mayfield Publishing Company, 1984.

Kamm, Thomas. "Bolivians Fear a U.S.-led War on Drugs: American Army's Presence May Set Off Violence." *Wall Street Journal*, June 24, 1991, p. A8.

Kawell, Jo Ann. "The Addict Economies." *NACLA* 22:6 (March 1989), pp. 33–38.

Kelley, Jonathan, and Klein, Herbert. *Revolution and the Rebirth of Inequality*. Berkeley: University of California Press, 1981.

Lanza, Gregorio. "Policia, Fuerzas Armadas, y trafico de drogas." *Presencia* (La Paz), April 28, 1990.

Lee, Rensselaer III. "Dimensions of the South American Cocaine Industry." *Journal of Interamerican Studies and World Affairs* 30:2–3 (Summer/Fall 1988), pp. 87–103.

Levine, Michael. *Deep Cover: The Inside Story of How DEA Infighting and Subterfuge Lost Us the Biggest Battle of the Drug War*. New York: Delacorte Press, 1990.

Mabry, Donald. "The US Military and the War on Drugs in Latin America." *Journal of Interamerican Studies and World Affairs* 30:2–3 (Summer/Fall 1988), pp. 53–76.

MacDonald, Scott B. *Mountain High, White Avalanche: Cocaine and Power in the Andean States and Panama*. Washington Papers, no. 137. New York: Praeger, 1989.

MacLean Stearman, Allyn. *Camba and Kolla: Migration and Development in Santa Cruz, Bolivia*. Orlando: University of Central Florida Press, 1985.

Malloy, James M. "Authoritarianism and Corporatism: The Case of Bolivia." In *Authoritarianism and Corporatism in Latin America*, ed. by James M. Malloy. Pittsburgh: University of Pittsburgh Press, 1979.
Migdal, Joel S. *Strong Societies and Weak States: State Societies Relations and State Capabilities in the Third World.* Princeton: Princeton University Press, 1988.
Mirtembaum, Jose. "Frente a la militarización consideramos la legalización." Unpublished paper, 1990.
Morales, Edmundo. *Cocaine.* Tucson: The University of Arizona Press, 1989.
Nadelman, Ethan A. "Cops Across Borders: Transnational Crime and International Law Enforcement." Ph.D. dissertation, Harvard University, Department of Government, June 1987.
Oporto-Castro, Henry. "Bolivia: El complejo coca-cocaina." in *Coca, cocaina, y narcotráfico: Laberinto en los Andes*, ed. Diego García-Sayán. Lima: Comisión Andina de Juristas, 1989.
Painter, Michael. *Institutional Analysis of the Chapare Development Project (CRDP).* Institute for Development Anthropology, Clark University, Worcester, Massachusetts, and Institute for Development Anthropology, Binghamton, New York, 1990.
Parks, Evelyn. "From Constabulary to Police Society: Implications for Social Control." In *The Criminologist: Crime and the Criminal*, ed. Charles E. Reasons. Pacific Palisades, Calif.: Goodyear Publishing Company, 1974.
Quintana Jaldin, Hugo. "Incumplimiento de leyes ocasionó la fuga de 4 narcotraficantes en menos de 24 dias." *Ultima Hora* (La Paz), May 22, 1990.
Quiroga, José Antonio. "Paradojas de una responsabilidad compartida." *Nueva Sociedad* (Caracas), no. 102 (July-August 1989), p. 169–172.
Rasnake, Roger N., and Painter, Michael. *Rural Development and Crop Substitution in Bolivia: USAID and the Chapare Development Project.* Cooperative Agreement on Human Settlements and Natural Resource System Analysis, Institute for Development Anthropology, Clark University, Worcester, Massachusetts, and Institute for Development Anthropology, Binghamton, New York, 1989.
Sage, Colin. "Drugs and Economic Development in Latin America: A Study in the Political Bolivian Economy of Cocaine in Bolivia." In *Corruption, Development, and Inequality*, ed. Peter M. Ward. London and New York: Routledge, 1989.
Sainz, Monsignor Luis, La Paz archbishop. *Presencia* (La Paz), March 3, 1990.
Schoultz, Lars. *National Security and United States Policy Toward Latin America.* Princeton: Princeton University Press, 1987.
Sharpe, Kenneth E. "The Drug War: Going After Supply." *Journal of Interamerican Studies and World Affairs* 30:2–3 (Summer/Fall 1988), pp. 77–85.
Taylor, Michael. *Community, Anarchy, and Liberty.* Cambridge: Cambridge University Press, 1982.
Trebach, Arnold. *The Great Drug War.* New York: Macmillan Publishing Company, 1987.
Vannett, Casey. "DEA Boss Authorizes Bolivians to Investigate Alleged DEA Abuses." *Times of the Americas*, June 12, 1991, p. 2.

Van Wert, James. "The US State Department's Narcotics Control Policy in the Americas." *Journal of Interamerican Studies and World Affairs* 30:2–3 (Summer/Fall 1988), p. 1–18.

Walker, William III. *Drug Control in the Americas.* Rev. ed. Albuquerque: University of New Mexico Press, 1989.

Watzlawick, Paul; Beavin, Janet; and Jackson, Don D. *Teoria de la comunicacion humana: Interacciones, patologias, y paradojas.* Translated from English by Carlos E. Sluzki. 3d. ed. Buenos Aires, Argentina: Editorial Tiempo Contemporaneo, 1974.

Wertheimer, Alan. *Coercion.* Princeton: Princeton University Press, 1989.

Wisotsky, Steven. *Beyond the War on Drugs: Overcoming a Failed Public Policy.* Buffalo, N.Y.: Prometheus Books, 1990.

Yates, Douglas T., Jr. "Hard Choices: Justifying Bureaucratic Decisions." In *Public Duties: The Moral Obligation of Government Officials.* ed. by Joel L. Fleishman et al. Cambridge, Mass. and London: Harvard University Press, 1981.

About the Book
and Author

The phrase "war on drugs" conjures up the weighty authority of the U.S. Army and the focus of its power on a tangible target. But *Smoke and Mirrors* reminds us that things are not always what they seem. It tells the story of a new Bolivian social structure, based on cocaine, composed of peasants manufacturing coca paste, wealthy merchants exploiting their labor and exporting the goods, and the so-called drug enforcers profiting from the drug trade. It weaves an intricate fabric made up of ordinary items—kerosene, car batteries, toilet paper—seized without question as drug-producing equipment; military barracks in the middle of the jungle; mock arrests and coca-paste burnings for important visitors; police officers chewing coca leaves to stay alert. This remarkable book, authored by a former secretary of state and solicitor to the Supreme Court of Argentina, reveals the ultimate paradox of the drug war: that drug enforcement is actually enhancing and perpetuating the cocaine trade in Bolivia.

Jaime Malamud-Goti, formerly state secretary and adviser in human rights and legal matters to former Argentine president Raúl Alfonsin, is currently Guggenheim Fellow in the Department of Anthropology at Columbia University. He is also professor and member of the Center for Advanced Studies at the University of Buenos Aires.